CW00509012

Business Language Practice

John Morrison Milne

Editor: Jimmie Hill

LANGUAGE TEACHING PUBLICATIONS
35 Church Road, Hove, BN3 2BE

© **LTP 1994**

ISBN 0 906717 54 X

The Author
John Morrison Milne is an experienced teacher of English for Business. He has worked in a number of countries including Sudan, Algeria, Greece, Spain, and Britain. He is currently working in Spain where he has specialised in teaching students in industry and banking.

The author would like to express his thanks to his colleagues at International House Executive Centre, Madrid, for their encouragement and help in piloting Business Language Practice. He is particularly grateful to his colleague Mohan Uddin for many suggestions and to his editors Jimmie Hill and Michael Lewis. He would also like to thank the following people for their help in producing pilot versions of the material: Sagrario Vicente, Victoria Baulenas, Susana Nunez, John and Nina Derkash, and, most of all, his wife Maria del Mar.

Note
All names and company names used in this book are fictitious and are not intended to relate to actual people or organisations.

Acknowledgements
Cover design by Anna Macleod
Cover photograph courtesy of Zefa
Cartoons courtesy of Punch
Typeset by Blackmore Typesetting Services, Brighton
Printed in England by Commercial Colour Press, London E7.

To The Student

Business Language Practice is a practical way for you to learn the English you need in everyday business situations – speaking, reading, or writing business English. Here is some advice to help you make the most of your studies.

1. Try to do the exercises regularly. Do one or two exercises every day. This is better than spending a whole evening once a week.

2. You will see that the book is in five sections: Speaking, Vocabulary, Grammar, Reading, and Writing. When you are working on your own, choose exercises from different sections.

3. Before you do an exercise, try to understand exactly what you have to do. Remember to read the instructions to each exercise carefully.

4. Remember that vocabulary is the most important thing in business English. This book teaches you about "word partnerships" – groups of words which occur together. Here are some examples:

    arrange a business trip   launch a new product

    take out a bank loan   foreign currency transactions

Always try to learn words in groups – not individual single words. We always use words together with other words – never alone!

5. When you do an exercise, always have a dictionary beside you – either an English-English dictionary, or a dictionary to help you translate what you do not understand. Try not to look up too many words – very often you can guess what something means.

6. There is an answer key at the back of the book to help you work alone. Always do the exercise first, THEN check your answers. It is quite common for some questions to have more than one correct answer. If you are in doubt, ask your teacher or an English-speaking friend or colleague.

7. Lastly, and most importantly, do not worry if you make mistakes. Mistakes are a normal part of the process of learning a language. If there are some mistakes which you make again and again, make a special note of them in a notebook. Remember the famous rule of business:

"The person who never made a mistake never made anything."

Contents

━━━━ *unit 1* ━━━━
Speaking: Introduction

1 Choose the best answer(s) to the questions. Use the spaces for your own answers:

1. Who do you speak to in English in your job?
   a) customers
   b) colleagues
   c) suppliers
   d) ....

2. Do you use English mainly
   a) face-to-face
   b) by fax or letter
   c) on the phone
   d) ....

3. How often do you have to attend meetings in English in your job?
   a) every day
   b) once a week
   c) twice a week
   d) rarely

4. What is your role in meetings?
   a) mainly speaking
   b) controlling the meeting
   c) listening and taking notes
   d) ....

5. How often do you give presentations?
   a) once a week
   b) occasionally
   c) once or twice a month
   d) never

6. How often do you welcome visitors to your company?
   a) once or twice a week
   b) occasionally
   c) once or twice a month
   d) never

7. How often do you need to use your English at work?
   a) every day
   b) occasionally
   c) once or twice a month
   d) never

8. How do you feel about your English?
   a) I feel relaxed and confident.
   b) I read very slowly.
   c) I am nervous on the phone.
   d) ....

Some expressions to use with an English-speaking visitor:

> **I'm afraid I don't speak much English.**
> **My English is a bit rusty.**
> **Could you speak a little more slowly?**
> **Could you repeat that please?**

2 Match the sentences on the left to the replies on the right.

1. Shall I ask her to call you back?	A And the name is...?
2. Can I get you some coffee?	B Oh, I just stayed at home. What about you?
3. Diana, can I introduce you to Mr Keiyama?	C Of course, please take a seat. Mrs Chandar won't be long.
4. I'd like a single room for two nights.	D Hello, I'm Diana Mason. I've heard a lot about you.
5. Hello, Jenny. How was the weekend?	E Yes, let's get down to business.
6. Right, shall we get started?	F Can it wait? I'm a bit busy at the moment.
7. My name's Karin Eckland. I've got an appointment with Mrs Chandar at 10.30.	G Yes, please. I'll be in my office till half past five.
8. Paul, can you just check these sales figures for me?	H That's very kind of you. Black, please. No sugar.

1		2		3		4		5		6		7		8	

3 Use these verbs to complete the conversations:

finish   **speak**   **know**   **get**   **tell**   **leave**

1. Could I .... to Mr Smith, please?
   > I'm sorry. He's just gone out.

2. Why did Jim .... the company?
   >He got a better offer from TLK.

3. Excuse me, can you .... me where the Marketing Department is?
   >Yes, take the lift to the second floor and it's on the right.

4. Do you .... Martina Polensky?
   > No, I don't think we've been introduced.

5. What time do you usually .... work?
   >It depends how busy we are. Usually after seven.

6. Can I .... you another drink?
   >Thank you. That's very kind of you.

4 Use these words to complete the gaps in the sentences.

last   **meeting**   **here**   **busy**
flight   **department**   **company**   **time**

1. What .... did you say it was?
2. Well, I'm rather .... just now.
3. Yes, of course, ... you are.
4. I'm afraid she's in a .... at the moment.
5. No, I'm in the sales .... now.
6. No, I was here .... year for the computer fair.
7. How was your .... , Jane?
8. Sorry, could you repeat the name of your .... ?

5 Now use one sentence from exercise 4 to complete each conversation.

1. Is this your first visit to Amsterdam?
   >..
   Yes, of course. I remember now.

2. Excuse me. Can I borrow your newspaper for a moment?
   >..
   Thank you very much.

3. So you're still working in marketing, Henri?
   >..
   Really. And how are you finding it?

4. HSA Computers. Can I help you?
   >Yes, please. Could you put me through to Mrs Shastri?
   ....

"Roy only plays really because it helps him with his business contacts."

5. ....
   >Yes, it's Rackham Electronics.
   And could you spell that for me, please?

6. Do you mind if I interrupt you for a second?
   >..
   I'm afraid it is rather urgent.

7. ....
   >It's half past seven.
   Thank you.

8. ....
   >Well, my plane was rather late taking off.
   Shall we go straight to your hotel then?

■ *unit 2* ■
Hello and Goodbye

1 Mark each of the following expressions in two ways:

F = formal   or   I = informal

B = beginning or   E = ending

1. Hi, Karen. How are you?
2. I'll see you later, then.
3. Good afternoon, Mr Trent.
4. I'm afraid I really must go.
5. Thanks for all your help.
6. Pleased to meet you.
7. Thank you for everything, goodbye.
8. Very well, thank you.
9. Not too bad.
10. Good morning, Mr Hashemi.
11. Well, I'd better be going.
12. What kind of weekend did you have?

F	I	B	E

2 Choose from the expressions in exercise 1 to complete these conversations:

1. ....

    >Good afternoon, Julie. Are there any messages for me?
    Yes, I've left them on your desk.

2. I've got a meeting at two o'clock.
    >Fine. ....
    Yes. I'll probably see you this afternoon.

3. ....

    >Fine thanks, and you?
    .... A bit busy, though.

4. Hello, Martine. ....
    >Quite busy. I had to work on Saturday, you know.

5. ....
    >Already?
    Yes, I'm afraid so. I'm seeing Jim at half past three.
    >Well, ...
    You're welcome.

3 Choose from the words below to complete the gaps in the dialogues.

fine	**people**	**later**		**good**	**busy**	**Morning**
afraid	**very**	**better**		**Hi**	**weekend**	**enjoy**

Dialogue 1

Rashid:	.... , Jane.
Jane:	Hi, Rashid. How are you?
Rashid:	.... thanks, and you?
Jane:	Oh, not too bad. Did you have a good .... ?
Rashid:	Yes, it was .... relaxing. I went to the theatre on Saturday.
Jane:	Did you .... it?
Rashid:	Yes. It was great.

Dialogue 2

Frank:	.... morning, Mrs Jansen.
Mrs Jansen:	.... Frank. How are you?
Frank:	Oh, very .... as usual. There's a letter for you.
Mrs Jansen:	Thanks very much, Frank. Well, I'd .... be going. I've got a lot of work to do.
Frank:	Bye.
Mrs Jansen:	See you .... , Frank.

4 Put the sentences in the conversations in the correct order.

Dialogue 1
a) Well, I'll leave you to finish it. See you later.
b) Morning Paul. How's everything?
c) That's right.
d) Hi, Lena. Not too bad. I'm quite busy as you can see.
e) Bye, Lena. And don't work too hard!
f) You're still working on the CDX report, I suppose.

1		2		3		4		5		6	

Dialogue 2
a) Good. Are there any messages for me?
b) Bye.
c) Good morning, Alicia. How was your weekend?
d) Yes, there's one here from Mr Hassan of Midtech. Can you phone him as soon as possible?
e) Oh. I just stayed at home and relaxed.
f) I'll do that. See you later, Alicia.
g) Good morning, Mrs Svensson.

1		2		3		4		5		6		7	

▰▰▰ *unit 3* ▰▰▰
First Meetings

1 Complete the gaps in the conversations below with the following:

introduce   met   this   first

heard   think   Pleased (2)   Hello   before

Conversation 1

Enrico: Gina, have you .... Thomas Goldman?
Gina: No, I don't .... so.
Enrico: Well, let me .... you. Tom, ... is Gina Piccolo. Gina's head of our marketing department.
Tom: .... to meet you, Gina. I've .... a lot about you.
Gina: All good, I hope!

Conversation 2

Hashim: .... I'm Hashim Kamil. I'm with the ARP group.

Trudi: .... to meet you. I'm Trudi Peters. I'm in the sales department here. Is this your .... trip to Canada?

Hashim: No, I've been here once ....

2 Now put the words in order to form expressions you can use when you meet someone for the first time:

1. Wilson   I'm   Hello   Tom

    ....

2. you   last   It's   meet   at   good   to

    ....

3. we   I   we've   before   don't   met   think

    ....

4. call   Wilson   I'm   Please   me   Tom   Tom

    ....

5. much   so   you   heard   I've   about

    ....

6. offices   like   I'd   our   you   to   new   all   welcome   to

    ....

3 Choose from the following words to complete the conversations. You will not need all the words.

business	meet	telling	colleague
visit	decide	couple	week
heard	successful	met	nice

Conversation 1

Jim: Teresa, I'd like you to .... Mahmoud. Mahmoud's our production manager in Cairo.

Teresa: .... to meet you at last, Mahmoud. I've .... quite a bit about you.

Mahmoud: Nothing terrible, I hope.

Teresa: Oh, no! Jim's been .... me that your plant has just introduced the new quality control system.

Mahmoud: Yes, it's been very .... so far.

Jim: Right. Shall we get down to .... then.

Conversation 2

Lisa: David. Have you .... Eleni Mavrou? Eleni is sales director of Torimed.

David: Hello.

Eleni: Is this your first .... to Greece, David?

David: Oh, no. I've been here a .... of times. In fact the last time I was here I met a .... of yours, Costas Lambidis.

4 Choose from these expressions to complete the conversation:

our marketing director	how do you do	two or three weeks	I don't think
have you met	Very slowly	our New York branch	I'll introduce you

Alex: Frances, ... Nina Hansen?

Frances: No, ... we've been introduced.

Alex: Well, if you come with me .... Nina, this is Frances Grey, ... Nina is in charge of the Florida project.

Frances: ....

Nina: Pleased to meet you.

Frances: How is the project going, by the way?

Nina: .... , I'm afraid. I've no idea when we'll be finished.

Study Tip Nowadays *How do you do* and *Pleased to meet you* are rather formal. In many introductions people simply say *hello*.

unit 4
You and Your Company

1 Choose from these words to complete the gaps in the conversation:

software   heard   free   meet

introduce   company   exactly   employee

Lisa:	Excuse me. Is anyone sitting here?
Louise:	No, it's .... Have a seat.
Lisa:	Thank you. Are you here for the marketing seminar?
Louise:	That's right.
Lisa:	Let me .... myself by the way. My name's Lisa Moran. I'm marketing director with BDT Products.
Louise:	Pleased to .... you. I'm Louise Swan.
Lisa:	So, you're in marketing too.
Louise:	Not .... I work more on the product development side. I'm R+D director with Hilmex. You might have heard of us. We're a small .... producer.
Lisa:	Yes, I've .... the name. You make the Deskworld series, don't you?
Louise:	Yes, that's us.

2 Now use information from the conversation to complete the first two columns. Complete the third column with information about yourself.

Name	Lisa	Louise	
Company			
Work Area			
Job			

3 Use your own information to complete the conversation below:

Paula:	Let me introduce myself. My name's Paula Winter. I'm with WTR.
You:	....
Paula:	Pleased to meet you. So you're in management training too?
You:	....
Paula:	Really? Who do you work for?
You:	....
Paula:	Oh. What kind of company is that?
You:	....
Paula:	That sounds really interesting.

4 Use these words to complete the gaps:

call	**flying**	**moved**	**research**
produce	**months**	**department**	**involve**

1. That's right. We .... integrated circuits.
2. No. I .... to Rome last month.
3. Quite a lot, yes. In fact, I'm .... to Paris tomorrow.
4. Gina Moretti. She joined us six .... ago.
5. What does your job actually .... ?
6. That's right. I work in the accounts ....
7. Yes. But we .... it "human resources" now.
8. I'm doing some .... on the Nigeria market.

5 Complete these short dialogues with phrases from Exercise 4.

1. So, you're in finance, Tom.
   > ....
   Well, let's hope you are solvent!

2. Do you travel a lot in your job?
   > ....
   Lucky you!

3. ....?
   > A bit of everything really. From promotions to accounts.

4. Who is in charge of sales now?
   > ....
   I've heard she's excellent.

5. What are you working on at the moment, Louise?
   > ....
   Of course. It's one of your main markets, isn't it?

6. So Norcon is an electronics company?
   > ....
   Then you're just the person I need to talk to!

7. Are you still based in Milan, Daniel?
   > ....
   Don't you miss all your friends?

8. Maria, you're still in personnel, aren't you?
   > ....
   I don't understand why they changed the name.

unit 5
Making an Appointment

1 Diane Kerr works for Intertrust, a large investment company. This is a page from her diary. Use these partnerships to complete the gaps:

meeting at Scotbank	collect tickets	from Hong Kong branch
check restaurant booking	remember to phone	from finance department

14. Monday/Lundi/Montag	**15. Tuesday/Mardi/Dienstag**
8 .... Henri in personnel to arrange meeting	8 check if fax machine has been repaired
9	9
10 visit from Kees Willems (RTP) 10.15	10 .... with Ann Lawson to discuss financing of TLC project
11	11
12 meeting with Chan Ling .... (12.15)	12
13	13 lunch with Thomas Herber (........)
14 Leslie .... wants to talk about new accounting procedures.	14 be back in time for meeting with Tom Kennedy 2.30
15	15
16 rest of afternoon free	16 phone Theatre Royal (remember to ....)
17	17

2 Now put this conversation in order:

A   Mr Willems, of course. Miss Kerr will be with you in a few minutes.

B   Yes, please. Black, no sugar.

C   Good morning. Can I help you?

D   That's all right. I don't mind waiting.

E   Please sit down. Can I get you some coffee?

F   Yes, my name's Kees Willems of RTP. I've got an appointment with Diane Kerr at 10.15.

1	
2	
3	
4	
5	
6	

3 Look at the dialogue below and put the words in the correct order:

Receptionist: you   good   help   I   can   afternoon

....?

Tom: to   an   got   Mrs Kerr   two   I've   at   yes   half   see   appointment   past

....

Receptionist: you   your   give   please   could   me   name

....

Tom: Kennedy   Dataplan   it's   Tom   from

....

Receptionist: long   Mr Kennedy   be   won't   she

....

Tom: don't   I   that's   waiting   mind   OK

....

4 Now use one word to complete the gaps in the dialogue.

waiting	appointment	would	somebody
see	afraid	kind	sorry

Receptionist: Good morning.
Caroline: Good morning. I've come to .... Mrs Kerr.
Receptionist: Have you got an .... ?
Caroline: .... ?
Receptionist: Have you arranged to see Mrs Kerr?
Caroline: No, I'm .... not. Is it inconvenient?
Receptionist: Well, she's with .... at the moment. If you don't mind
                .... , I'll ask her if she can see you.
Caroline: That's very .... of you.
Receptionist: .... you like some coffee while you wait?

5 Mark each of the following expressions   P = polite or R = rude

1.   I'm afraid Mrs Kerr is still in a meeting.
2.   No, you can't see her now. She's busy.
3.   I want to see Mrs Kerr now, if you don't mind.
4.   Would you mind waiting for a couple of minutes?
5.   Sit down. I'll see if she's got time to speak to you.
6.   I'm afraid the meeting's taking a bit longer than expected.
7.   No, I can't wait. I've got an important meeting.
8.   Look, I've got no idea when she'll be back.

▬ *unit 6* ▬
Meetings

1 These word partnerships are missing from the memo. Can you put them in the right gap?

International Marketing   **remember to bring**
look forward to seeing   **a copy of the agenda**
latest developments   **give you a ring**

Hi, Louise,

This is .... for today's meeting at 11.30. I hope you'll manage to be there. It would be nice if you could say something about the .... in the TRX7 project. Raju from .... will be there and I know he'll be interested in what you have to say.

Could you also .... your copy of the Milan report as we're going to talk about it (point 3 on the agenda). I'll .... later to confirm the details.

I .... you at 11.30.

Tom

2 Put these sentences in the correct gaps:

I'll pass on your apologies to the others.
Yes, it's sitting here on my desk.
I just hope you get your problems sorted out.
I see. How long will it take to repair?
Hang on, Louise. I'll just put you through.
Really? What's the matter?

"Business is really terrible – we're supposed to be a tax-loss."

Louise: Morning, Eleni. Is Tom there by any chance?
Eleni: ....
Tom: Hi, Louise. Did you get my memo about this morning's meeting?
Louise: ...., but I'm afraid there's a small problem.
Tom: ....
Louise: Well, there's been a breakdown on the assembly line. Production has stopped completely.
Tom: ....
Louise: Two or three hours at least. So I'm afraid I'll have to miss the meeting.
Tom: That's a pity. Anyway, ...
Louise: Thanks, Tom. I knew you'd understand.
Tom: That's OK. ....
Louise: Me too.

3 People often make excuses when they cannot attend a meeting or when they are late. Look at the pictures and complete these excuses:

1. I'm afraid I can't make today's meeting. I'm ....
2. I may be late for this morning's seminar. I've got ....
3. Sorry I'm late. I was ....
4. I'm sorry I couldn't go to your presentation yesterday. I ....
5. Paula's just phoned. She says ....

4 Choose from these verbs to complete the sentences below. Remember to use the correct form of each verb:

take   send   have   chair   get   discuss   call   receive

1. I've .... this meeting to talk about the changes to our overtime policy.
2. Karen can't come to this morning's meeting. She .... her apologies.
3. Can we .... started? I don't want to be here all day.
4. I've asked Jens to .... the minutes at today's meeting.
5. There are four main points to .... today.
6. Can we .... a short break now?
7. Has everyone .... a copy of this morning's agenda?
8. The MD was ill so Henri had to .... the budget meeting.

Some useful expressions at meetings:

Can we go over that last point again?

Sorry, I'm not quite clear about what you said.

Could we go back to point 3 on the agenda for a moment?

5 Can you add more verbs which go with MEETING.

1. call a meeting
2. attend a meeting
3. cancel a meeting
4. arrange a meeting

5. ....
6. ....
7. ....
8. ....

unit 7
On the Telephone 1

1 Use these expressions to complete the gaps in the mini-dialogues.

> Certainly. It's V-O-G-E-L.
> Just a second. I'll get a pen.
> Speaking.
> Yes. Could I speak to Denise Martin, please?
> Yes, of course. It's Karin Vogel.
> Sorry, who did you want to speak to?
> Do you know his extension number?
> "Marsen". With an "M".
> "Marsen Electrics".
> Yes. But I got his answering machine.

"Mr Pointman, while you were out, a Miss or a Ms or a Mrs Valdy or Volney or Balmy left a garbled message for you."

1. RCL Electrique. Can I help you?
   > ....
   Just a moment. I'll put you through.

2. Could I speak to Harry Pavlidis, please?
   > ....
   Harry Pavlidis. In the sales department.

3. Could I speak to Ludmilla Korschka, please?
   > ....
   Ludmilla! I've been trying to ring you all morning.

4. Sorry. Could you repeat the name of your company?
   > ....
   Is that with "N" or "M"?
   > ....

5. Did you manage to ring Phil?
   > ....

6. Could I leave a message for Teresa?
   > ....

7. Could you give me your name, please?
   > ....
   Sorry. Could you spell your surname.
   > ....

8. Could you put me through to Pete Lensky, please?
   > ....
   No, I'm afraid I don't.

2 Use the following words to complete the sentences on the left. Then match each one to the most appropriate response on the right.

calling	department	say	time
extension	repeating	fax	back

1. Who shall I say is ....?
2. Can you give me your .... , please?
3. Would you mind .... that, please?
4. Sorry. Did you .... Kellman?
5. Marketing .... .Can I help you?
6. .....and your .... number is?
7. Can you tell her I'll phone .... later?
8. What .... do you normally open?

A Yes, could I speak to Mrs Elliot?
B I'm afraid we don't have a fax machine
C Usually between nine and half past.
D Yes, I said the WX342, leaving at 16.25.
E Yes, I'll pass on your message.
F Yvonne Simon of Northam Insurance.
G Let me check. Yes, it's 461.
H No, "Kellerman", with two 'l's.

1		2		3		4		5		6		7		8	

3 Choose from the phrases below to complete these two telephone conversations:

Conversation 1

was just going to	Can I	speaking
Could I speak	I'm phoning to check	put you through

Witan International. .... help you?
> .... to Mrs Weiss, please?
One moment, please. I'll ....
>Kristina Weiss ....
Good morning, Mrs Weiss. This is Ellen Johanssen from Ostlink Travel. .... if you got my letter.
>Yes, I've just received it. In fact, I .... ring you. There are a couple of things I wanted to ask you about...

Conversation 2

I'm afraid	This is	I'll ring back
Can I help you?	Could I speak to	I'll just see

RCL Electrics. .... ?
>Yes, ... Kristina Weiss of Witan. .... Denise Martin, please?
.... if she's available... No, ... she's just popped out.
>In that case, ... later.
Who can I say phoned?
>Oh, it's all right. I'll phone back.

unit 8
On the Telephone 2

1 **Put a verb in each space to complete the conversations. Remember to use the correct form of the verb:**

Conversation 1

Receptionist:	Witan International. Can I .... you?
Sanjay:	Could I .... to Mrs Weiss, please?
Receptionist:	Who's .... please?
Sanjay:	Sanjay Rahman of LRN Technical.
Receptionist:	Sorry. What did you .... your name was?
Sanjay:	Mr Rahman of LRN Technical.
Receptionist:	Could you .... your name for me?
Sanjay:	R-A-H-M-A-N. Sanjay Rahman.
Receptionist:	Of course, Mr Rahman. I'll .... you through.

Conversation 2

Julia:	Sales. Julia Wells ....
Paolo:	Morning, Julia. This is Paolo Ferrei from BRN. I'm .... to find out if you .... my fax.
Julia:	Hold on. Let me .... a look. No I don't think so. When did you .... it?
Paolo:	This morning. It should have .... by now.
Julia:	I'll check again and .... you back later.
Paolo:	Fine. I'll .... in the office till half past twelve.

2 **One of the most difficult things to do on the phone is to end a call. Here are eight possibilities. Some could be rude. Mark the polite ones with a (P) and the rude ones with an (R).**

1. I must get back to work. Goodbye.
2. I'd better go. I've got a lot of work to do.
3. Don't worry. I'll give you a ring tomorrow with the details. Goodbye.
4. I must stop this call now. Goodbye.
5. It's been nice hearing from you. I'll be in touch. Goodbye.
6. I'm too busy to go on talking. I'll try to ring you tomorrow.
7. I'm a bit busy this morning. Is it OK if I ring you later?
8. OK. I'll look forward to hearing from you on Monday. Goodbye.
9. Let's leave it at that then. Goodbye.
10. I can't spend all day talking to you. Goodbye.

3

Sometimes it's not easy understanding people on the phone. Here are some expressions that might make things easier:

Sorry, who did you say you wanted to speak to?

I can't hear you. Could you speak up?

Which department did you want?

Could you speak more slowly, please?

Use an appropriate expression to complete the gaps:

1. Receptionist: LRN Technical. Can I help you?
   Paula: Could I speak to Mr Rahman, please?
   Receptionist: ....
   Paula: Sanjay Rahman. In finance.

2. Bill: ...and the order is for 370 AS3 cables and 35 JF1 switching units.
   Paula: ....
   Bill: Sorry. I do tend to speak too fast. I said: 370 AS3 cables and 35 JF1 switching units.

3. Receptionist: Sorry. ....
   Paula: Marketing, the marketing department.

4. Eleni: So we'll change the meeting to two o'clock on Friday?
   Paula: .... There's a lot of noise here.
   Eleni: I said: let's have the meeting at two o'clock on Friday.
   Paula: OK, agreed.

"Are you in or out?"

4

Put the sentences in the correct order to make a conversation:

A I'm afraid she's in a meeting at the moment.

B Thank you. Goodbye.

C I see. Well, can you ask her to call me back?

D I'll make sure she gets your message, Mr Paved.

E Hersch Trading. Can I help you?

F Can you give me your name, please?

G Could I speak to Mrs Elliot, please?

H I'm Rajit Paved of Central Power. My number is 215 56 78. Could she ring me some time this afternoon?

1	2	3	4	5	6	7	8

▬▬▬ *unit 9* ▬▬▬
Leaving a Message

1 Use these partnerships to complete each of the gaps in the answerphone recordings.

Sorry I'm not here	**on Saturdays**	**is closed**	**after the tone**
as soon as I get back	**for calling**	**leave a message**	**opening hours**

1. Thank you .... TDK Products. I'm afraid that our office .... and there is no-one to take your call at the moment. Our .... are 08.30 - 18.30, Monday to Friday, and 09.00 - 12.00 .... Please leave your name and number ...., and we will get back to you as soon as possible.

2. This is Phil Thomas. .... at the moment to take your call. If you'd like to ...., please speak after the tone. I'll ring you ....

"Hello. Mr Portman's answering machine is on the fritz. This is his parrot.
Leave your name and number and I'll have him get back to you."
(on the fritz = out of order. Am. Eng.)

2 Here are two messages left on an answerphone. Fill in the gaps with these words:

repeat	**machine**	**fax**	**possible**	**trying**
ring	**check**	**ask**	**urgently**	**that's**

1. This is Paula Ricci of Velex Supplies. I need to speak to Diana Winter of Sales. Can you .... her to .... me first thing tomorrow morning? My number is 071 237 9897, ... 071 237 9897. I'll just .... my name: Paula Ricci of Velex Supplies. Oh, and could you tell her that I got her .... about the Turin Conference?

2. Phil, this is Janine. I've been .... to ring you all day but all I get is the answering .... Where have you been? I need to speak to you .... about the Belman contract. I've had a look at it and there are a couple of things we need to .... before we send it out. Can you ring me as soon as .... ? I'll be here till about half past seven. Bye.

3 Match up the notes by your secretary and the actual message:

NOTES   **MESSAGES**

1. Middle East order still trouble.   _____

2. Ring your brother.   _____

3. PS/1s out of stock. Try another supplier?   _____

4. If EBM ring back, tell them I've re-faxed the payment details.   _____

5. German flight now leaving half an hour later.   _____

6. Hussein sends his apologies.   _____

MESSAGES

A   Ted. It's Bill. I must speak to you urgently. Ring asap.

B   This is EBM - the accounts department. Your fax was unclear. Please send it again.

C   Could you make sure this message gets passed on to the Developments Group. Mr Hussein can't make the meeting tomorrow. He is very sorry, but something has come up which he cannot get out of.

D   This is Pumps International of Abu Dhabi. Our order of 22nd May stilll has not arrived. Please investigate and call us back as soon as you can.

E   This is Computerworld. We are temporarily out of stock of PS/1s. How urgent is your order?

F   We have made a mistake with the departure time of Mr Hoskins flight to Munich. It is now departing Toulouse at 16.15, new E.T.A is 17.45 at Munich.

4 Now find words in Exercise 3 to complete the following:

1. If you are asked to reply 'asap', this means ....
.... In other words it is ....

2. The .... time of a plane is the time when it leaves. If someone talks of its ....,
they mean its estimated time of arrival.

3. If you cannot supply goods because you have none left, it means you are ....
.... If this is only for a short time, the problem is only ....

4. If you cannot attend a meeting, you send your ....

▬*unit 10*▬
Socialising

1 Use these sentences to complete the gaps in the conversations. Be careful. There is one extra sentence.

Let me show you some of the sights.
I don't have anything planned.
Some other time, maybe?
Are you enjoying the conference?

Do you fancy a quick jog round the block?
Would you like to join us?
Fine. That'll give me time to get changed.

INTRODUCING

Tom: You've met Kate, haven't you?
Sue: Yes, we met at this morning's marketing seminar.
Tom: We're going out for a drink. ....
Sue: Yes. That sounds nice.
Kate: Let's go then.

INVITING

Pat: What are you doing this evening, Jules?
Jules: ....
Pat: I'm going out for a meal with some people from our Toronto branch. Why don't you come with us?
Jules: Great. I'd love to.
Pat: Well it's half past six now. Let's meet in the bar at eight o'clock.
Jules: ....

REFUSING

Sarah: Would you like to join us for a drink, Henri?
Henri: I'd love to but I'm a bit tired. It's been a long day.
Sarah: ....
Henri: Yes, why not tomorrow evening?

SUGGESTING

Ben: Is this your first visit to Montreal, Lisa?
Lisa: Yes, I haven't found my way around yet.
Ben: ....
Lisa: Are you sure we have enough time?
Ben: Yes, the next session doesn't begin till two o'clock.
Lisa: Fine, let's go then.

Yoko: You're up early, Sue!
Sue: I always go out for a run in the morning. ....
Yoko: No thanks. Far too energetic for me.

2 Choose from these verbs to complete the gaps in the note. Remember to use the correct form of each verb:

> meet   write   hope   give   join   send   see   make

Dear Alice,

I ....your product presentation went well. A group of us are going out for a meal this evening. Would you like to .... us? We're .... downstairs in the main reception area at quarter past eight. .... me a ring and let me know if you can .... it. Hope to .... you later.

Carol

"Do say if there's anyone you don't know."

BANX

3 When you meet business colleagues socially, you often want to talk about other things - family, holidays, hobbies etc. Here are 12 ways to start a conversation on such topics. Match them up with their responses.

1. Are you married?

2. Do you have a family?

3. Does your wife/husband work?

4. Are your children still at school?

5. Are you having a holiday this year?

6. What are taxes like in your country?

7. Are houses expensive where you live?

8. I hate all this travelling on business, don't you?

9. The conference seems very well-organised, doesn't it?

10. What do you do when you're not working?

11. What kind of food do you like?

12. Are you doing anything later this evening?

A   Yes, we're off to Florida.

B   Anything really, but I'm very fond of Chinese.

C   No. I'm not actually. What about you?

D   It depends really. In the city centre they are, but prices have remained fairly stable for the past few years.

E   Golf - I'm a fanatic! Four rounds most weekends. What about you?

F   Yes, two boys and a girl - what about you?

G   Yes, (s)he's an architect.

H   Too high! Same as everywhere!! No, seriously, income tax isn't too bad, but VAT is now over 20%

I   Very well-organised, isn't it - much better than last year's.

J   Yes - sleeping. See you tomorrow.

K   Yes, one's at school and the other's at University.

L   Yes and no - I like seeing different countries.

1		2		3		4		5		6		7		8		9		10		11		12	

unit 11
Vocabulary: Introduction

The best way to increase your business vocabulary is to learn more words and more groups of words - word partnerships. Here are some examples.

1. May I make a suggestion?

    You can also make *a decision, a proposal, an appointment*.

2. It's a very successful company.

    A company can be *successful, important, growing,* or *long-established*.

3. Did you get my memo about the sales meeting?

    You can *get* a memo, *send* a memo, *reply to* a memo, or *file* a memo.

1 Here is a short text. Some of the word partnerships are *in italics*. Can you underline some of the others?

My name's Gabrielle Meier. I work for GRC Transport, *a medium-sized, transport firm* based in Groningen, Holland. *At the moment* I work in the personnel department though I've also worked in sales and finance. I enjoy my work because *it gives me a chance* to meet people and to deal with problems on an everyday basis. It's a friendly company to work for and there's a good working atmosphere. We all know each other and *we get on well*. The other thing I like about my job is that it gives me the opportunity to travel; next week I'm going to a training conference in Italy.

2 Now use a word partnership from the text to complete the gaps in these sentences:

1. In my job I .... problems which come up in the export department.

2. I .... very well with my boss. In fact we're more friends than colleagues.

3. I took the job because it gives me .... to five or six different countries every year.

4. No, I'm afraid Mrs Ellis is in a meeting .... Can you ring back in half an hour?

5. I spend most of my days working alone with the computer. My job doesn't give me much of .... to get out and ....

3 Complete the following with information about yourself. Then underline any useful word partnerships.

I work for .... It's a .... company/organisation based in .... Our main products/services are .... I work in the .... department/section, and I deal with .... I enjoy my work because..................................... .

Study Tip Remember when you meet a new word, try to find out what other words go with it - its partnerships. The partnerships are just as important as the word itself.

4 It will help if you can organise your vocabulary notebook so that you learn word partnerships rather than lists of single words. Here are some examples related to travel:

      business trip   **travel expenses**   **economy class**

      travel agent   **direct flight**   **jet lag**

Use a partnership to complete each sentence:

1. I'm afraid there's only one .... per week from here to Boston. Normally, you have to go via New York.
2. We don't make our own travel arrangements. We use a .... which specialises in dealing with companies like ours.
3. Many companies make their staff travel .... nowadays to save money.
4. Alice is away on a .... at the moment. She'll be back on Wednesday,
5. My flight from New York only got in at half past seven this morning. I'm still suffering from ....
6. Don't forget to claim your .... when you get back from Manila.

5 One type of partnership that is very common in modern business English is the noun + noun combination, for example:

      transport firm   **personnel department**   **training conference**

How many partnerships can you make from these columns? There are at least 20.

sales	costs
transport	problems
bank	manager
management	department
production	line
software	consultants

Use these partnerships in the following:

1. I've just been to see my .... about a new loan.
2. Our computer operators are having an in-service training day run by a firm of ....
3. Our distribution people have been experiencing a lot of .... recently.
4. We called in a .... to try to solve some of our organisational problems.
5. Our whole .... had to close down yesterday due to an electrical fault.

6 In the exercise below underline the verbs which you can use correctly with each noun. Two verbs in each group do *not* form partnerships:

1.	post, get, work, receive, send, deal	A LETTER
2.	make, copy, return, expect, send, take	A CALL
3.	call, return, attend, cancel, post, have	A MEETING
4.	arrange, cancel, make, send, get, book	A TRIP
5.	deal, give, offer, expect, buy, increase	A DISCOUNT
6.	hold, run, visit, represent, sell, deal	A COMPANY

7 Complete the sentences by choosing one or more word partnerships. For example, in no 1 both a and b are correct.

1. Did you .... I sent yesterday?

   >Yes, I did.
   a) receive the fax   b) get the fax   c) fax me   d) fax machine

2. Can I speak to ...., please?
   > I'm afraid she's in a departmental meeting at the moment.
   a) the sales manager   b) the sales target   c) the sales management   d) the sales team

3. Telcan Pacific is .... company, isn't it?

   a) management potential   b) a leading service   c) a rapidly expanding   d) in charge of

4. Can I open .... at this branch?

   >Yes of course. Can you fill in this form?
   a) a bank manager   b) a cheque book   c) a current account   d) a savings account

5. Do you have much .... ?

   >Yes. I've worked in the field for the past four years.
   a) sales experience   b) experience in sales   c) sales staff   d) sales account

6. Where would you prefer to have lunch?

   > Is there a .... restaurant near here?
   a) good French   b) French cooking   c) traditional English   d) cheap Italian

7. I am writing to you .... your letter of June 12th.

   a) in touch with   b) in reply to   c) in response to   d) after replying

8. .... everyone in the department I'd like to express my thanks to Mrs Reiss for her contribution to the project.

   a) on my part   b) by name of   c) on behalf of   d) by the name of

9. So what do you think about Carol?

   > She seems quite ....
   a) good working   b) a hard worker   c) work harder   d) hard working

10. I'm afraid we'll have to limit this year's .... to 2.5% because of the economic conditions.

    a) wage rise   b) salary increase   c) pay rise   d) pay increase

Study Tip When you find new word partnerships, remember to write them down as well as single words.

━━unit 12 ━━
In the Office

1 Complete the words below with the vowels a, e, i, o, u. All the words are common office objects:

1. st _ p l _ r
2. d _ s k _ t t _
3. c _ l _ n d _ r
4. s c _ s s _ r s
5. p _ p _ r c l _ p
6. n _ t _ p _ d
7. c _ l c _ l _ t _ r
8. d _ s k d _ _ r y
9. d r _ w _ r
10. r _ b b _ r s t _ m p
11. f _ l d _ r
12. _ n v _ l _ p _

2 Use these word partnerships to complete the gaps.

blank diskettes   **a pair of scissors**
in the bottom drawer   **borrow your calculator**
pass me my diary   **for this envelope**

1   22.6 x 33.25? I'm useless at mental arithmetic. Can I .... for a moment?
>Here you are. Let me just switch it on for you.

2. Can you remember what time we're meeting Mrs Rainer tomorrow?
>.. and I'll have a look. Yes, it's ten thirty.

3. Harry, have you got an "airmail" sticker .... ?
> Have a look in my desk. They're .... on the left.

4. Excuse me. Have you got .... ?
>Yes, here you are. Be careful. They're a bit sharp.

5.   Have you got any ....? I want to back up this work.

3 Match a verb to a noun to make word partnerships.

1.	answer	A	a staff meeting
2.	book	B	the sales figures
3.	attend	C	a couple of letters
4.	check	D	the printer
5.	order	E	the phone
6.	post	F	a visitor
7.	repair	G	a hotel room
8.	greet	H	some photocopy paper

1		2		3		4		5		6		7		8	

4 **Now choose partnerships from Exercise 3 to complete the following conversations:**

1. If you're going out can you .... for me?
    >Yes, of course. Have they got stamps?

2. Paul. Can you remember to .... ? I think we've almost run out.
    > No, I'm sure there's another box or two downstairs.

3. Can someone .... ? It's been ringing for the past five minutes.
    > I'll get it.

4. Are you all set for the Osaka conference?
    > Well, I've sorted out my flight but I still need to ....

5. Isn't anyone coming to .... ?
    > No. I phoned the technician and he says that all it needs is a new ink cartridge.

6. I think we'd better .... again. I'm sure there's a mistake somewhere.
    > I looked at them this morning and I couldn't see anything wrong.

5 **Use these verbs to fill in the gaps in the notes:**

give	**return**	**let**	**lend**	**know**	**do**
leave	**get**	**have**	**make**	**need**	**meet**

1. Morning Alice,
    Sorry to rush you but I .... the revised price list this morning, preferably before 11
    o'clock. If I'm not in my office, just .... it on my desk. *Louise*

2. Louise,
    Sorry I was late with the list. You .... how busy we've been in sales in the past few
    days. If you've any questions just .... me a ring. I'll be around till 5.30. *Alice*

3. Hi Paul,
    Did you .... a chance to read my report on the Warsaw venture? Could we
    .... some time later today to talk about it? I'll be free till half past two. *Corinne*

4. Dear Corinne,
    Today's impossible, I'm afraid. Can we .... it tomorrow morning instead? Say, ten
    o'clock or ten thirty? Just .... me know what time is best for you. *Paul*

5. Dear Alex,
    Could you .... me a big favour? Could you possibly .... me your lap-top for
    a day or two? I promise I'll look after it. *Luke*

6. Hi Luke,
    My lap-top's in the top drawer on the right. I've also left the manual in case you ....
    any problems. Could you .... it before the weekend? *Alex*

Now look at the notes again and underline some word partnerships.

unit 13
Company Departments

1 Match the departments on the left with the correct definition on the right:

1.	sales	A	is responsible for manufacturing goods
2.	purchasing	B	deals with recruiting new staff
3.	planning	C	deals with invoices and payments
4.	research and development	D	handles advertising and new product launches
5.	quality control	E	buys in products and services
6.	production	F	tries to develop new products
7.	personnel	G	makes sure that standards are maintained
8.	finance	H	persuades people to buy the company's products
9.	distribution	I	sets out a strategy for the company's future
10.	marketing	J	transports goods to different places

1		2		3		4		5		6		7		8		9		10	

2 Use the spaces below to write a short description of your department:

I work in the .... department/section. There are .... people working in this department. Our main tasks are .... and .... We also .... I deal with ....

"The man we need must have guts, daring and initiative, Mrs. Hempson! Is your son that man?"

3 Underline the verbs which form partnerships with these nouns. Two verbs do not make partnerships in each example.

1.	make, ask, design, buy, meet, market, sell	A PRODUCT
2.	visit, fax, keep, work, lose, market, meet, help	A CUSTOMER
3.	give, meet, improve, offer, market, ask, sell	A SERVICE
4.	run, give, visit, manage, sell, operate, develop, make	A FACTORY

4 In the extracts below some managers of ABEX, a Lagos-based manufacturing company, are describing their departments. Use the words below to complete the gaps in the extracts and write the names of the departments in the spaces provided.

background	recruiting	supervise	maintain
biggest	standards	consumers	sacking
responsible	scientific	technical	launching
check	improving	shifts	questionnaires

1. Robert Ngara

In my department we're .... for making sure that .... know about our products. We also deal with .... new products. We use .... and surveys to find out what products people want to buy.

Robert is head of the................................ department.

2. Hassan Abdelkader

Our department is the .... in the company. In fact there are over 250 of us altogether, and most of the people work in a system of three .... Our work never really stops, unless there are .... problems. One of my main jobs is to .... part of the assembly line.

Hassan is a supervisor in the .... department.

3. Tessa Mkrana

We work very closely with Hassan's department although there are fewer of us. One of our most important tasks is to .... items on the assembly line to make sure there are no problems. We have to .... very high .... in the factory. I also liaise with our principal customers to make sure there are no problems.

Tessa is head of the .... department.

4. Hafiz Ahmed

Mine is the smallest department in the company. In fact there are only five of us and we all come from a .... or engineering .... Basically what we do is to devise new products or to look at ways of .... the products we make at the moment. It's a very exciting job.

Hafiz works in the .... department.

5. Tamara Oku

I work in the "human" side of the business. My department is involved in .... new staff, training them, and dealing with a whole range of problems, including personal problems. I suppose that's why some people refer to our activities as "human resources". And the part of my job I don't like? Well, it's me who's in charge of .... people if their work is not up to standard.

Tamara works in the .... department.

unit 14
Describing a Company

1 Look at these extracts and underline the partnerships used to describe companies and departments.

Novokrin, the leading Danish pharmaceuticals group, has announced plans to restructure its rapidly expanding medical supplies division.

A leading management consultant has urged managers in state sector enterprises to introduce more productivity bonuses for workers.

The Indian government has said that it will hold an inquiry into allegations that one of the country's top manufacturing companies breached import regulations last year.

Hamburg-based steelmaker, Siegel Werke, has announced plans to sell its loss-making aluminium division after failing to reach an agreement with unions.

2 Now use these partnerships to complete the gaps:

Florida-based	**biggest employers**
family run	**highly profitable**
food distribution groups	**pharmaceutical company**
loss-making manufacturer	**chemicals division**

1. UTLChem, a top Dutch .... , has just announced plans to introduce a new pain-killing drug onto the market.

2. UTLChem is a .... company. Last year it announced earnings of over $50m. This was an increase of 15% over the previous year.

3 It is also one of the area's .... Over 2,000 people work for the firm, most of them in the production division.

4. The group's fast-expanding .... contributed more than a quarter of total profits last year.

5. Vendasur, one of Mexico's largest .... , has just announced a takeover of the Redman Canning Company.

6. Siltex is still a .... firm. The present chairman, Paul Sanders, is the grandson of the company's founder.

7. Simon Schluter, a .... company with its headquarters in Miami, has announced plans to expand into Mexico and South America.

8. CETA Products, the .... of car components is to close its main production centre after earnings fell dramatically in the second half of the year.

3 Use these partnerships to complete the dialogue. You will not need all the partnerships:

two main divisions   **on the publishing side**   **in the pipeline**
about 500 people   **directly under**   **fairly diversified**

Frank: So how do you like your new firm, Jean?
Jean: Great. It's a .... company called Selmar.
Frank: I see. What kind of company is it?
Jean: It's part of a group. There are .... - paper production and publishing.
Frank: That sounds interesting. Which area are you in?
Jean: I'm .... - in charge of book distribution in France and Belgium.
Frank: It's a big operation, I suppose.
Jean: You're right. There are .... in publishing. I've got 25 people
.... me.
Frank: And what about the future?
Jean: Oh, there are big expansion plans .... We're moving into North America next year. And after that, who knows?

4 Read this description of a company and complete the information below:

Micropol AT is a highly profitable software company, with a workforce of over 1,000 and an annual turnover of $300 million. Its main products are applications programs for industry as well as for educational institutions. Its many customers include small and medium-sized companies, government departments as well as students.

The company was founded in Santa Monica, California, in 1978. The original founders, Karen Sawyer and Lee Heng, were still students when they went into business. Their idea was only to earn some extra money. Micropol began to grow rapidly and by 1980 turnover was over $4m.

Initially the company worked in the area of Software Consulting. However, in 1982 Sawyer and Heng introduced the first version of the Adword wordprocessing program. It was an immediate success. Students liked it because it was easier to use than other programs on the market.

In 1985 Lee Heng left Micropol and set up his own company, Intertrack. Karen Sawyer is still Company President and thinks that Micropol has a bright future. The company has ambitious plans. Later this year it will launch a new version of its DataPol database program. There are also plans for a joint venture with Kaito, the leading Japanese computer firm.

Name of Company ....

Activities ....

Workforce................................... Location .... Turnover ....

Profits .... Market .... Plans ....

5 Use word partnerships from the text above to complete this description:

KLT Industrial .... in Gröningen, Holland, in 1954. Originally the company manufactured household goods, but nowadays its .... are office furniture and equipment. The group's service division offers a wide range of business services from cleaning to waste disposal. The current ...., Robert Moers, is the son of the founder. He has .... for KLT. For example, the company is going to put a new range of ergonomically-designed furniture .... early next year. Dr Moers is also negotiating a .... with German electronics giant DK Hoffman.

Look through the texts again and underline word partnerships.

══*unit 15*══
The Business Trip

1 In the two columns match the words on the left with those on the right to make word partnerships about travel.

1. business
2. expense
3. duty
4. time
5. excess
6. boarding
7. hand
8. taxi
9. departure
10. travel

A baggage
B difference
C class
D claim
E free
F fare
G lounge
H luggage
I agents
J card

1		2		3		4		5		6		7		8		9		10	

2 Now use some of your partnerships from exercise 1 to complete these dialogues:

1. What's the .... between here and New York?
    > Six hours, I think.

2. Allan, can I give you this .... for my trip to the States?
    > Sorry, but I don't deal with expenses now. You have to go to Kate in finance.

3. If you've got a moment, Di, can you ring the .... and book me a seat on the morning flight to Geneva?
    >You'll be flying .... as usual, I suppose?

4. Can I see your ...., sir?
    >Yes, of course. Here you are.
    Is that bag yours?
    >Yes it is.
    I'll have to put it in the hold, I'm afraid. You're only allowed one piece of .... in the cabin.

5   Thanks for the perfume, Tom. It must have cost a fortune.
    > Well, actually, I bought it in the .... shop at Athens airport.

6. By the way, how much is the .... from the airport to your office?
    > About $15, I think. It depends on the route the driver takes.

3 Which of the verbs form partnerships? Two of the verbs in each do not fit.

1. catch, take, book, travel, miss, fly, reserve, choose   an EARLY FLIGHT
2. catch, book, leave, run, change, reserve, choose   a HOTEL ROOM
3. arrange, make, travel, plan, cancel, catch, delay   a BUSINESS TRIP
4. book, miss, change, buy, collect, mislay, catch   a PLANE TICKET

4 Use these verbs to complete the sentences.

> hire   check in   change   meet   confirm   stay   miss   land

1. You must phone the airport to .... your flight 24 hours before departure.

2. Passengers for Turin should ....at the Alitalia desk.

3. If you wish to .... a car on landing, please speak to one of our ground staff on arrival.

4. It's best to .... your money before you leave for the States. You'll get a much better rate here.

5. Don't worry, Martina. I'll arrange for our driver to .... you at the airport and take you to our office.

6. Look, it's nearly eleven o'clock. If we don't get a move on we'll .... our flight.

7. If I'm in Singapore, I usually .... at the Royal Park Hotel.

8. What time does your flight .... in Brussels?

5 Choose from the partnerships below to complete the article.

1. a) bigger chairs   b) wider seats   c) better furniture
2. a) frequent flyer   b) common passenger   c) usual traveller
3. a) first thought   b) decided first   c) first introduced
4. a) only 200 miles   b) every 200 miles   c) either 200 miles
5. a) economics class   b) economy class   c) economical class
6. a) interest free   b) duty free   c) free flights
7. a) hotel residence   b) hotel visits   c) hotel accomodation
8. a) round-the-world   b) whole world   c) wide world

Flying business class offers the busy executive many advantages. The airlines advertise their ...., superior menus, exclusive departure lounges and many other features. Now many business travellers are being tempted by a new attraction: business travel programmes. These offer the .... bonus points for each flight he or she takes with the airline.

The idea was .... by a number of airlines in the United States, but it now seems to have caught on in other parts of the world. Canada's Air Intercontinental recently introduced its own Flight 201 Programme which offers passengers a bonus mile for .... they fly in business class.These programmes are aimed very clearly at business and first class passengers rather than at tourists. Points are given only to those who pay full fare. Passengers in .... do not qualify for extra miles. Internal flights are also excluded.

Most of those lucky enough to qualify for the programmes exchange their bonus points for .... for themselves and their families. Some airlines also offer ...., car hire facilities and even clothing. One executive recently exchanged his points for a .... trip on Concorde, while another used hers to treat her family to a week-long stay in Disneyland.

unit 16
Describing Your Product

1 Here are 8 products:

A a car	B a television	C a lap-top computer	D whisky
E a shirt	F a magazine	G a photocopier	H a chair

Use the following phrases to complete the descriptions. Then match a product with its description.

latest technology	short-sleeved	high-quality	with ice
remote control	small enough	hard-wearing	fast-changing

1. The DS3 can make over 100 copies a minute. It uses A3 or A4 paper and provides a clear, ... image. It's simple to operate and needs very little maintenance.

2. The new DF2 MicroCom 486 DX-33. .... to carry with you and powerful enough to handle the most sophisticated software. So don't wait. Call your nearest MicroCom dealer today.

3. Over 60 pages of fact and opinion every week. Our team of journalists keep you informed of the latest developments in today's .... business world. Order your copy today.

4. Matured for 12 years at our Glenfillan distillery, it is a luxury everyone can afford. We use only the finest barley and purest Highland spring water so you can enjoy it by itself or ....

5. The new TR 800 is ideal for the executive on the move. Its powerful engine, aerodynamic design and comfortable interior make the journey shorter. We've used the .... to get you there on time.

6. Designed for today's office, the Executive ST3 is the ultimate in comfort. Upholstered in .... fabric, the ST3 comes in a choice of three colours. You'll find it's simply the best.

7. Perfect for work or leisure. It's made of 100% light Indian cotton with reinforced collar and cuffs. Long-sleeved or .... , it comes in four sizes, extra-large, large, medium and small.

8. Simply the sharpest, crispest picture and the clearest sound. Our new model has a high resolution 50 x 70 cm screen and DLX stereo speakers. With its one-touch .... operation it couldn't be easier to use.

2 Use these words to complete the gaps in the questions:

deliver	models	price	available
cost	discount	market	information

1. What kind of .... could you offer us?
2. Does the .... include delivery?
3. Can you give me some more .... about it?
4. How much does it .... ?
5. When can you .... to our factory?
6. How many .... do you currently produce?
7. How long has it been on the .... ?
8. Is it .... in other colours?

3 Now use the questions in exercise 2 to complete this dialogue:

....?

There are four versions of the TX4 on the market at the moment. If you look at our catalogue you can see that the top of the range is the TX4 1A.

....?

> Just over four years. It's still one of our biggest sellers despite the competition from Enatech.

....?

> Yes, but at the moment only in white or grey. We're bringing out a model in red next year.

....?

> That depends on the model you order. This one currently costs £600 excluding VAT.

....?

> Again, it depends. We normally offer 15% off catalogue price for orders of 20 units or more.

....?

> No, I'm afraid it doesn't. You'll have to pay extra for deliveries outside London.

....?

> If you fax your order to us we can have the goods at your factory gate in less than 24 hours.

....?

> Well, if you look at the catalogue I sent you last week you can see that...

4 In many situations we use the partnership "not very" plus a positive adjective to express a negative idea.

So, instead of saying or writing: **The TXC4 is a very unreliable printer.**

We prefer: **The TXC4 is not very reliable.**

Now change these sentences using "not very" and one of the following adjectives:

      efficient   user-friendly   good   cheap   profitable   polite

1. The Adfile X2 program is very difficult to use.
   > I agree. It's ....

2. And it is very expensive.
   >Yes. You're right. It's ....

3. And the after-sales service is really bad.
   > ....

4. They take a long time to answer calls.
   > ....

5. And the staff are so rude!
   > ....

6. I'm not surprised the company's losing money.
   > ....

5 Cross out the two adjectives which are not normally used to describe the following:

1. fast, expensive, reliable, rude, new, expanding, safe, stylish   A COMPANY CAR
2. easy, friendly, user-friendly, useful, strong, new, difficult   A COMPUTER PROGRAM
3. heavy, expanding, user-friendly, important, small, difficult   A MARKET
4. reliable, efficient, small, product, safe, established, sure   A COMPANY

unit 17
The Working Lunch

1 Put these foods into the correct category:

chicken, potatoes, lamb, scampi, steak, broccoli, lobster, salmon, peaches, beef, apples, octopus, haddock, cabbage, prawns, cod, onions, pears, ham, tomatoes, crab, trout, brussels sprouts, oranges, pork, spinach, turkey, carrots, herring, grapes, mussels, squid, duck, plums, veal, pheasant.

fish	seafood	meat	poultry	vegetables	fruit

2 What is the opposite? Use these adjectives:

mild   cold   well-done   alcoholic   sparkling   light   dry   stale

1. a heavy meal ....
2. fresh bread ....
3. spicy food. . ...
4. still water ....
5. sweet wine ....
6. hot soup ....
7. a soft drink ....
8. rare steak ....

3 Use these verbs to complete the gaps in these useful sentences:

book   order   bring   recommend   follow   eat
have   prefer   start   ask   suit   take

1. Do we have to .... a table or can we just turn up?
2. I've ordered a table for half past twelve. Does that .... you?
3. Would you like something to drink or shall we .... straightaway?
4. Can I .... the garniture de légumes? It's one of the chef's specialities.
5. I think I'll have the aubergine salad to .... and the salmon to ....
6. Which do you .... - red or white?
7. I'm a vegetarian. I don't .... meat or fish.
8. No dessert for me, thanks. I'll just .... coffee.
9. Would you like anything else or shall I .... for the bill?
10. Could you .... us the bill, please? Do you .... Visa?

4 Use these verbs to complete the following:

love   take   get   eat   try   have   find   fancy

1. I'll .... a mineral water, please.
2. I .... curry too spicy.
3. Do you .... something to eat?
4. Let's .... the Taj Mahal for a change.
5. I .... there fairly often.
6. I .... Mediterranean food.
7. Can I .... you something to drink?
8. How long will it ....?

5 Now use the sentences in exercise 4 to complete these conversations:

Planning the meal

Tom: Right...?
Gina: Good idea. I'm quite hungry actually.
Tom: Where would you like to go?
Gina: Well, you know London much better than me.
Tom: ....
Gina: What kind of place is that?
Tom: It's our local Indian restaurant.
Gina: Oh, I'm not very keen on Indian food. ....
Tom: Do you like Greek or Italian food?
Gina: Yes, ...
Tom: What about the Kerkyra? It's a small Greek restaurant. It's only five minutes' walk from here.
         ....
Gina: That sounds fine.

In the restaurant

Tom: A table for two, please?
Waiter: I'm afraid you'll have to wait. We're rather full today.
Tom: ....?
Waiter: Only five or ten minutes. ....?
Tom: What would you like, Gina?
Gina: ....

6 Use these words to complete these conversations:

sounds	recommend	follow	menu	bill
order	starter	wonderful	pay	seafood

The Menu

Tom: Could we have the ...., please?
Waiter: Certainly, sir. Here you are.
Tom: Thank you.
Gina: Well, what do you ...., Tom?
Tom: Let's see. You could try the dolmades as
         a ....
Gina: What's that like?
Tom: It's very nice. It's a spiced rice dish wrapped
         in vine leaves.
Gina: That .... fine.

Ordering

Waiter: Are you ready to .... yet?
Tom: Yes, we'll have the dolmades to begin.
Waiter: And to .... ?
Tom: I'll have souvlakia. And you, Gina?
Gina: Let's see. What's kalamarakia like?
Waiter: It's a .... dish. Made with squid.
Gina: Well, I'll have that.

Paying

Tom: Could I have the .... please?
Waiter: Yes, of course.
Tom: Can I .... by cheque?
Waiter: Certainly, Sir. Can I see your card, please?
Tom: Have you enjoyed your meal, Gina?
Gina: Yes, it was .... We must come here again.

"Let me see, tomorrow he's having a working breakfast, a working lunch and a working dinner . . . in between he's playing golf."

▰*unit 18*▰
Banking

1 **Many verbs form partnerships with money words. Complete the gaps in these sentences with these verbs. Use the correct form of each verb:**

invest	**lend**	**lose**	**owe**	**make**
keep up	**save**	**earn**	**spend**	**take out**

1. If you take out a loan, make sure you can .... the repayments.
2. The bank manager refused to .... us the money we needed. She said that our accounting system was too disorganised.
3. Diana has really done well since she moved to the States. She .... more than $80,000, and she has a company car.
4. We've decided to move to a new office to .... money. The place we rent at the moment is too expensive.
5. Since I got my credit card I've .... far too much money.
6. Scotbank decided to close its Tokyo operation because it was .... money.
7. I wish I hadn't .... that loan. I still .... the bank £3,000. I don't know when I'll be able to pay it back.
8. The easiest way to .... money is to .... wisely in the Stock Market.

2 **Use these verbs to complete these word partnerships about banking.**

use   pay   cash   change   open   make

1. .... a current account
2. .... two hundred dollars
3. .... this cheque
4. .... bank charges
5. .... a bank transfer
6. .... the cash dispenser

Use these word partnerships to complete the following:

7. I'd like to ....
   > Of course. If you go over to the foreign desk someone will help you.

8. Excuse me. Can I .... ?
   > Certainly. Could you sign it on the back and date it, please.

9. I've just moved here. I'd like to ....
   > Certainly. Would you mind filling this form in. There is a minimum deposit of £20.

10. So with this new Scotbank Plus account the customer gets free banking?
    > Not exactly. You .... if your account is overdrawn.

11. Don't the banks close at three o'clock around here?
    >Yes, but you can still .... to withdraw money.

12. I'd like to ....
    > How much would you like to send?

3 **Use these words to complete this letter from a bank to its small business customers:**

financial	services	fortnightly	charges	staff
interest	branch	location	currency	range

Dear Customer,

We are delighted to announce the opening of a new city centre .... of Scotbank at 34 Market Street. In our new convenient .... we are ready to offer all the banking .... the small business needs:

- expert........................ advice tailored to your company's needs
- a wide .... of credit facilities for the expanding business
- highly competitive .... rates
- highly professional .... ready to attend to your every banking need
- fast, efficient foreign .... transactions.
- the lowest bank .... you'll find anywhere: ask about our new free banking facility
- regular account statements - weekly or ....

So don't hesitate. Come to Scotbank and speak to our manager, Sarah Wilson. You'll wonder why you ever banked anywhere else.

Yours sincerely,

JC Forrest
Marketing Director

4 **Use these partnerships to complete the gaps in the conversation between the bank manager and a customer:**

moved my account	cash flow forecast
in business	borrow some money
some more information	profit and loss account

Manager: So you'd like to .... to expand your business, Mr Carson?
Customer: That's right, Mrs Wilson. Initially, we need a loan of £25,000.
Manager: You haven't banked with us very long, have you?
Customer: No, not really. I only .... to Scotbank two months ago.
Manager: Of course I'll need .... about your company before I can give you an answer.
Customer: Well, it's a fairly new company. We've only been .... for a year and a half.
Manager: And you're in the speciality foods business?
Customer: That's right. We supply restaurants and delicatessens in the area.
Manager: Fine. Now let's have a look at your company's finances.
Customer: I've brought along some figures for you to study. This is our latest .... and here's a current balance sheet.
Manager: That's fine. I'll also need a .... for the next six months.
Customer: Really? What's that exactly?
Manager: It's a projection of how much capital your company will need over the period. And of course, I'll need some time to think about this.
Customer: Well, I would appreciate a fairly quick decision.

▬▬ *unit 19* ▬▬
Numbers

1 Match the figures and the words on the right.

1.	2,400	A	two hundred and fifty six
2.	-18°C	B	eleven point five percent
3.	256	C	fifteen square metres
4.	16th	D	twenty four point three six
5.	15m²	E	between thirty four and thirty seven percent
6.	34-37%	F	two thousand four hundred
7.	10.55am	G	three and a half million
8.	2.987	H	sixteenth
9.	11.5%	I	forty seventh
10.	3,500,000	J	oh eight one three four seven two nine eight
11.	tel 081 347 298	K	minus eighteen degrees centigrade
12.	15m³	L	fifteen cubic metres
13.	24.36	M	twelve pounds fifty
14.	6 x 7 = 42	N	five to eleven in the morning
15.	£12.50	O	six times seven equals forty two
16.	47th	P	two point nine eight seven

1	2	3	4	5	6	7	8	9	10	11	12	13	14	15	16

Now cover the right side of the page and see if you can pronounce the numbers.

2 Can you give the following answers in full:

1. The unemployment rate in your country. ....

2. Your country's current inflation rate. ....

3. The number of people working in your company. ....

4. Interest rates in your country at the moment. ....

5. The average temperature in July. ....

6. The population of your town/city. ....

7. The cost of a kilo of coffee. ....

8. The average rent of a small flat in your country per month. ....

9. The population of your country. ....

10. The telephone number of the Fire Brigade in your country. ....

3 Look at these articles from the Press.

JOB LOSSES

LTC Industries, the Belgian food processing group, has announced plans to reduce its workforce. The company currently employs 1,200 people, 800 at its Antwerp production centre and the rest at its Bruges headquarters. It is thought that LTC plans to cut about 20% of the total workforce. The biggest cuts will be in production which employs 600 workers.

TOURISM UP 5%

The Spanish Ministry of Tourism has reported that almost 30,000,000 foreign tourists visited the country in the first 6 months of this year. This is an increase of about 5% over the figure for the same period last year. Earnings from tourism were estimated at over $8bn, a rise of 25% over last year's figures. July was the busiest month with a total of 9,000,000 visitors.

BETTER NEWS

The Stock Market closed slightly higher last night after a busy day of trading. More than 2,000,000 shares were traded in the course of the day, the highest figure for three months. Most of the interest was in the banking sector where 250,000 shares changed hands. Shares in First National Bank last night stood at $4.80, an increase of a third since the beginning of the year.

PRICES SLASHED

CompuTex, the leading manufacturer of personal computers, has announced plans to cut the prices of many of its products. Prices of its leading ManTex PC range will fall by around a fifth, the ManTex 400 PC now costing £1,000. The company's printer range is unaffected by the decision.

Now say if these sentences are true or false:

1.	One third of LTC's staff work at the company's headquarters.	T/F
2.	More than 300 workers will lose their jobs.	T/F
3.	About half the workforce is employed in production.	T/F
4.	Last year 25 million tourists visited Spain.	T/F
5.	Income from tourism rose by $2bn.	T/F
6.	More than a third of tourists came in July.	T/F
7.	One eighth of shares traded yesterday were in banking.	T/F
8.	Shares in First National Bank were worth $4.20 at the beginning of the year.	T/F
9.	Many CompuTex products will be 20% cheaper.	T/F
10.	The prices of CompuTex printers will fall by 25%.	T/F

4 Use the spaces to write these figures in full:

1. 3,456 ....

2. 23.64% ....

3. 2½ ....

4. 1 ¾ ....

5. 27m² ....

6. 3ft x 5ft ....

═══*unit 20*═══
The Verb 'get'

1 The verb GET is very important in business. It is used in many common word partnerships and idiomatic expressions. Use these GET partnerships to complete the gaps in the conversations:

get me a copy	get the fax
get used to it	get a taxi
get any idea	get a headache
get to the office	get that last point

1.   What time did you .... this morning?
     > Around eight o'clock. There was hardly any traffic.

2.   If I work with the computer for more than two hours I begin to ....
     > Why don't you use a protective screen? It's much safer.

3.   I'm sorry. I didn't quite .... Would you mind repeating it?
     > Well, I was just trying to explain why our Far East strategy is causing so many problems.

4.   While you're out, Paul, can you .... of the Financial Times?
     > Of course, Lisa. Is there anything else you'd like.

5.   Did you .... I sent you this morning?
     > Hang on. I'll just have a look. Yes, here it is.

6.   How are you getting on with the new Adword 2.5?
     > I'm not sure. It's a very difficult program to use.
     Don't worry. You'll soon ....

7.   I'm going to be late for my appointment with Yvonne.
     > You'd better ....

8.   Have you .... when Paula will be back?
     > No. I'm afraid she didn't say a thing.

2 GET is also used in many idiomatic expressions. Match the sentences on the left with the meanings on the right:

1.   Can we get a move on?   A a small party
2.   Why don't you get lost?   B unable to give my opinion
3.   The job's getting me down.   C hurry
4.   I couldn't get a word in at the meeting.   D making progress
5.   We're getting somewhere at last.   E go away please
6.   We're having a little get together.   F depressed and unhappy

1		2		3		4		5		6	

3 Now write some more GET partnerships in the spaces:

get ....   get ....
     ....
     ....

4 Underline the partnerships with GET in these sentences.

A   Did you get a chance to see the sights?
B   I didn't get home till after midnight.
C   We're not going to get a pay rise this year.
D   She gets over $50,000 a year and a company car!
E   So you're getting married in July, Paula?
F   Can I get you a coffee while you're waiting?
G   We'd better get her a present.
H   I got a phone call from her this morning.
I   I'm getting a direct flight to Hong Kong on Friday.
J   Right. Shall we get started, then?

5 Now use the sentences from exercise 4 to complete these conversations:

1.   ....
     > That's very kind of you. Black, please.

2.   Did you know it was Roula's birthday today?
     > No, I didn't. ....
     What about some flowers. She loves roses.

3.   ....
     > Don't you think we should wait for Henri?
     No, he's usually late. I'd rather get started now.

4.   How was your trip to Rome?
     > Very busy.
     ....

5.   How's Karen getting on in her new job?
     > She thinks it's great . ...

6.   Have you heard from Elena recently?
     >Yes. ....
     Really. How's she getting on in the new job?

7.   What time did the meeting finish?
     >Ten o'clock last night. ....
     You must have been exhausted.

8.   I thought you were going to the Osaka fair?
     >That's right. ....
     Then I'm flying on to Tokyo on Saturday evening.

9.   How are the salary negotiations going?
     > Very badly. ....

10. ....
     >That's right. I hope you'll be able to come to the wedding.

unit 21
The Verbs 'make' and 'do'

1 Use the correct form of MAKE or DO to complete the gaps:

1. Can you .... sure the proposal's finished by tomorrow?
    > I'll .... my best, but I can't guarantee anything.

2. Who are your biggest customers in Germany?
    > Well, we .... a lot of business with Sielman.

3. So, Paula's not very happy in her new job.
    > Apparently not. She's .... it clear she wants to leave the company.

4. How are you getting on with the new software, Martina?
    > Very well. In fact we've found we can't .... without it.

5. Are you .... a lot of money in your new job?
    > Not as much as I would like!

6. My boss isn't very happy with me. She says I just sit and .... nothing all day.
    > Why don't you have a word with her and explain?

7. Have you got a moment, Jules?
    > Just a second. I've got to .... a quick call to Louise at head office.

8. How's the Ukraine project going, Carl?
    > Very slowly. We haven't .... much progress since the end of July.

9. Roberto, can you .... a couple of extra hours this evening? I need some help
    with the Interbank proposal.
    > Well, actually, I was hoping to get home early.

10. Di, have you managed to finish the Interbank proposal yet?
    > Almost. I've .... most of the detailed figures. Roberto's still working on the text.

2 Underline your MAKE or DO partnerships from exercise 1. Complete these dialogues with the following six important ones. Use the correct form of the verb:

do the figures	**make progress**
do without	**make a call**
do my best	**make sure**

1. Olivier. Can I use your phone. I just need to .... ?
    > Of course. The phone's over there.

2. I'm just going over to head office. Do you need anything?
    >Yes. I've got a message here for Paul. Can you .... he gets it?

3. Are we .... much .... in the Middle East?
    > Yes, we're now the market leaders in 3 countries and we're doing very well in 2 others.

4. Are you coming to this morning's meeting, Louise?
    > I'll ...., but I can't promise. We're very busy with the accounts.

5. Have you finished the finance report yet?
    > I'm still .... for the last quarter, but I'll be finished in about two hours.

6. How's Juliet getting on in your department?
    > Very well. In fact we can't .... her now.
    Yes, I heard she was very good.

3 Complete the gaps with the correct form of DO or MAKE.

1. What are you .... this weekend?
2. DMK Trading .... a big profit last year.
3. I think you've .... a mistake here.
4. Have you .... those sales figures yet, Michel?
5. May I .... a suggestion?
6. Are you .... some more coffee, Jim?
7. She's gone to Paris to .... a computing course.
8. Could you .... me a favour?
9. We .... some market research last year.
10. No, I'd rather .... a start right away.

4 Now use some expressions from exercise 3 to complete these dialogues:

1. ....
    > Certainly, go ahead.
    I think we should target the Italian market.

2. ....
    > Certainly. What is it?
    Could you lend me a copy of the France report?

3. ....
    >Oh, nothing much. Probably staying at home.

4. I haven't seen Juliet for a while.
    > ....
    Of course. She told me she was going back to college for a couple of months.

5. Can I have another look at the proposal?
    > Of course. Here you are.
    ....
    >Really?
    Yes, you haven't included VAT in the total.

6. So you've decided not to launch the JUX2?
    > That's right.
    ...., and we decided that the market wasn't
    right at the moment.

7. ....
    > Yes, I've just finished. Here you are. Sorry it took so long.

8. Do you think we should wait for Roger?
    > ....
    I agree. We've wasted enough time as it is.

▰▰▰ *unit 22* ▰▰▰
Wordbuilding

1 Complete the columns below with the correct word. In the fourth column write a partnership with one of the words:

	Verb	Person	Activity	Partnership
1.	manage	....	....	*departmental manager* ....
2.	sell	....	....	....
3.	....	advertiser	....	....
4.	buy	....	....	....
5.	consult	....	consultation	....
6.	....	trainer/trainee	....	....
7.	present	....	....	....
8.	....	assistant	....	....
9.	....	....	employment	....
10.	operate	....	....	....
11.	....	....	advice	....
12.	consume	....	consumption	....
13.	....	....	dealing/deal	....
14.	produce	....	....	....

2 Choose words from those above to complete the following:

1. What do you think about this proposal from Smithson?
   > I .... you not to sign anything for the moment. At least not until you've studied it carefully.

2. So why did you decide to leave Franklin Industries, Marina?
   > I found it too inflexible. Most middle and junior .... didn't have any decision making powers.

3. How did the launch of Loxel shampoo go?
   > Very slowly at first. But after we introduced our television .... campaign sales began to take off.

4. Your sales reps seem very professional, Alice.
   > Yes. We give them a two month .... course before we send them out.

5. So, you're still interested in breaking into the Japanese market?
   > Of course we are! With over 120 million .... it's a vital part of our strategy.

6. I thought you'd sold your French subsidiary, Paul?
   > That was the plan, but we couldn't find a ....

7. You're looking pleased, Mike.
   > We've just signed a $4 million .... with GTF to supply them with accounting software.

8. Have you seen our new range of .... for the teenage market?
   > No, I didn't know they were even in ....!

3 Use the correct form of the word (in brackets) to complete the sentence:

1. We've decided to call in a firm of .... to prepare the market report. (consult)
2. Most of the .... team work on a commission basis. We find that it provides a greater incentive. (sell)
3. Sherman West, one of Europe's top .... agencies, ran a very successful campaign for our XL2 range. (advertise)
4. My personal financial .... told me not to invest in Hallet Industries. She warned me that the company was having serious cashflow problems. (advise)
5. Eleni's away at the moment. She's doing a two week .... course in Amsterdam. (manage)
6. May I introduce Kathy Lee? She's my secretary and personal .... (assist)
7. When our Japanese guests arrive, I'll make a short welcoming .... Then we'll go straight into the meeting. (speak)
8. Rashid worked as a switchboard .... for six months before moving to the general office. (operate)
9. Franklin Industries is one of the biggest .... in the region. Altogether they've got over 2,000 .... (employ)
10. If you write to us we will send you a list of Harman Computer .... in your area. (deal)

4 Use the correct form of the word in CAPITALS to complete each sentence.

1. APPOINT
   a) I've got an .... with Mrs West at half past ten.
   b) Haven't you heard that someone's been .... to the post of Promotions Manager?

2. ORGANISE
   a) What kind of .... do you work for?
   b) When I started working here the sales department was very .... Now it's a model of efficiency.

3. INTRODUCE
   a) Who's making the .... speech at the Annual General Meeting?
   b) I've read the .... to the report, but not the rest of it.

4. DEVELOP
   a) Kamel's in charge of Research and ....
   b) Our old head office has been bought by a firm of property ....

5. PRODUCE
   a) Sweden is an important .... of steel.
   b) Fresh farm .... must arrive in first class condition.
   c) The new VW mini-bus is now in ....

53

unit 23
Grammar: Introduction

1 It is easier to think about grammar if you know the names of grammatical forms. The exercises below help you with these grammar words, for example:

noun, adjective, verb, adverb

Match the underlined words in the sentences to the grammatical forms on the right:

1.	Did you speak to <u>the</u> sales manager.	A	personal pronoun
2.	I saw her <u>on</u> Monday.	B	question word
3.	Give <u>me</u> a ring some time tomorrow.	C	conjunction
4.	I think Paula <u>works</u> in the marketing section.	D	preposition
5.	<u>Could</u> I speak to Mrs Lee?	E	adverb
6.	It's a <u>friendly</u> company to work for.	F	modal auxiliary
7.	That's a <u>very</u> interesting suggestion.	G	definite article
8.	<u>Who</u>'s going to the meeting on Friday?	H	noun
9.	I'm afraid we never give credit to new <u>customers</u>.	I	adjective
10.	LKM closed down <u>because</u> exports fell away.	J	main verb

1		2		3		4		5		6		7		8		9		10	

2 Match the verbs underlined on the left to the tenses on the right:

1.	I'<u>m</u> still <u>waiting</u> for your sales report.	A	present simple
2.	<u>Has</u> anyone <u>used</u> this program before?	B	present continuous
3.	At ten o'clock we <u>were</u> still <u>arguing</u> !	C	present perfect
4.	She'<u>d</u> already <u>left</u> by the time I got to the office.	D	present perfect continuous
5.	I'<u>ll be</u> at head office till four o'clock.	E	past simple
6.	Delivery normally <u>takes</u> two or three days.	F	past continuous
7.	I <u>haven't been waiting</u> long.	G	past perfect
8.	We <u>tried</u> to break into the Polish market last year.	H	the 'll future

1		2		3		4		5		6		7		8	

3

Many words in English can be used in more than one grammatical category. Look at how <u>market</u> is used in these sentences:

It's an expanding <u>market</u>.	(noun)
BLZ is a <u>market</u> leader in Germany.	(adjective)
We're planning to <u>market</u> the IYR program.	(verb)

Look at the <u>underlined</u> words in the sentences below and say if they are nouns, verbs, or adjectives:

1. Who's going to <u>chair</u> this afternoon's meeting?   ....
2. Employees must feel they have <u>job</u> security.   ....
3. The <u>future</u> prospects of the company are excellent.   ....
4. Are there any hidden <u>costs</u>?   ....
5. Has this project been <u>costed</u>?   ....
6. Did you remember to <u>book</u> the seats?   ....
7. Olivier gave us a really interesting <u>talk</u> on the Taiwan market.   ....
8. We usually <u>number</u> those boxes to make identification easier.   ....
9. FL Bank of Zurich will <u>finance</u> the takeover.   ....
10. There's an <u>increasing</u> possibility that I'll be transferred.   ....

4

How do you feel about making mistakes in English? Do you worry about them or do you think they are a normal part of learning a language? Here are eight opinions from students. Tick (✓) the ones you agree with and put a cross (✗) against the ones you disagree with.

	AGREE	DISAGREE
1. I hate making mistakes. I feel so stupid.	☐	☐
2. I don't care if I make mistakes. The most important thing is that people understand me.	☐	☐
3. I get angry if I make a mistake. After all, I know the grammar rules. I hate repeating the same grammar mistakes.	☐	☐
4. I don't worry about grammar mistakes. Vocabulary mistakes are much more serious.	☐	☐
5. I don't usually know when I've made a mistake. And other people don't usually notice.	☐	☐
6. I wish other people would correct me more when I speak. I'm sure they laugh at my mistakes.	☐	☐
7. Pronunciation mistakes are the worst. Then people really don't understand you.	☐	☐

Study Tip Remember that a lot of incorrect language is successful and a lot of correct language is not successful. Think about it!

5

In each of these dialogues there is a common mistake. Underline the mistake, then write the correct English in the space.

1. So I'll see you at Monday, then?
    >That's right. At ten o'clock.
    ....

2. What means this word here?
    >I've got no idea. Have a look in the dictionary.
    ....

3. Do you still work with Frances?
    >Oh, no. She work in the personnel department now.
    ....

4. PEX Finance. Can I help you?
    >Could I speak to sales manager, please?
    ....

5. So, you're working for Teldata now?
    >That's right. It's the most big software producer in the country.
    ....

6. Who did write this report?
    >I think it was Roberto.
    ....

7. Was there many people at the telecommunications conference?
    >Yes. At least a thousand.
    ....

8. What happened to the new version of the BLX2?
    >We thought it would be successful, but any of our customers were interested.
    ....

"If the worst comes to the worst he can always go into his father's business, of course."

unit 24
The Articles: a/an, the

1 Complete the spaces using the correct article: *a, an,* or *the*.

1. Good morning. Let me introduce myself. My name's Tessa Lane, I'm .... accountant and I work for .... medium-sized industrial finance company in London. My company, Ajax Enterprises is one of .... most important manufacturers in .... country. We produce .... wide range of goods including plastics for .... automobile industry. I enjoy my job because it gives me the opportunity to meet lots of interesting people and to travel abroad. .... only thing I dislike about my job is having to work at .... weekend.

2. I got .... fax from Sigrid in Copenhagen this morning. She says she'd like to arrange .... meeting with us some time in .... next two months. Would you like me to give her .... ring and fix .... time?

3. I'm writing to ask if anyone in your company is interested in attending .... marketing conference in July. .... conference will be held in .... beautiful location near Paris. It will give your staff .... excellent opportunity to look at .... current state of some key European markets. We need to have .... firm decision by 30th March at .... latest.

4. .... Claymore is .... luxury hotel located close to Edinburgh's business centre. We provide everything you need for .... comfortable and successful stay in Scotland's capital. You need .... fax machine? We can install one in your room. You need .... important document typed or copied? No problem. We have .... pool of trained secretaries ready to assist. You have .... important meeting? Don't worry. Our international conference centre is equipped with .... luxury boardroom where business becomes pleasure. .... Claymore is Scotland's premier business destination. Give us .... ring today.

5. According to .... recent study, Swiss executives are still .... highest paid in Europe. .... report published by .... Simon Hartner Consultancy also puts Spanish executives among .... top earners. However, ... figures did not take into account perks like company cars and free medical insurance.

2

Uncountable nouns do not usually take the articles a/an.
We say: I study marketing.   Not: *I study a marketing.
However, in partnerships you often find an article:
I work for a marketing consultancy.

Put the nouns on the left with the correct partnership:

1.	finance	an	....	manual
2.	parking	an	....	column
3.	shopping	a	....	space
4.	instruction	a	....	dispenser
5.	information	a	....	jam
6.	cash	a	....	centre
7.	advice	an	....	desk
8.	traffic	a	....	house

3

Now use the partnerships from exercise 2 to complete the gaps in these conversations:

1. What time is Ruth coming?
   >She's going to be late. She's just rung to say that she's caught in .... in Manor Road.

2. What's Hasan doing now?
   >He's working for a computer magazine. He writes .... every month for readers with software problems.

3. So you leave your car in the street, Julie. Isn't that a bit dangerous?
   >Yes. But I haven't got ....

4. What happened to your old headquarters?
   >We sold the building to a firm of property developers. Now it's ....

5. Excuse me. Do you know where the marketing seminar's being held?
   >Sorry. I'm new here myself. I think there's .... in the reception area.

6. Can I use this card to withdraw money?
   >Yes. There's .... just outside the building. You can use it there.
   Thanks.

7. There's a part of this new budgeting programme I can't understand.
   >Didn't .... come as part of the software package?

8. The bank has just said no to our application.
   > Have you thought of trying .... instead?

══ *unit 25* ══
The Present Simple and Continuous

1 The verbs in the following sentences are either in the Present Simple or Present Continuous tense. Mark the Simple ones S and the Continuous ones C:

a)   I'm getting used to it.

b)   How long does it take to deliver to Manchester?

c)   Which other languages do you speak, Sven?

d)   We provide catering and cleaning for big companies.

e)   I'm trying to get through to Rashid Aziz in Accounts.

f)   I go abroad at least once a month.

g)   What are you planning to do in the holidays, Tom?

h)   I'm still waiting for a call from head office.

2 Now use the sentences to complete the gaps:

1.   So you travel quite often in your job, Maria?
     >Yes, that's right. ....

2.   ....
     >Russian and Japanese. And I also know a bit of Spanish.

3.   How are you finding the new database programme, Karen?
     >It was quite difficult at first, but now ....

4.   Are you coming for lunch, Roula?
     >I'll join you in about ten minutes. ....
     What? They haven't rung you yet?

5.   And what does your company produce?
     >Actually, we're a service company. ....

6.   ....
     >I'm not sure yet. We might go to Italy or even France. What about you?

7.   Velex Supplies. Can I help you?
     >..
     I'm afraid he's having the day off. Can I take a message?

8.   ....
     >Normally two or three days. But I can send it "express" if you like?
     Yes. I think that would be a good idea.

3 Use the following verbs in the Present Simple or Present Continuous to complete the text:

study   enjoy   work(x2)   live   manufacture   employ

Hello, my name's Maria Lascaratou. I was born on Skopelos, a Greek island and now I .... in Athens. No, not Athens, Greece, but Athens, Georgia, in the United States. My company, Scantech, ... components for the electronics industry. The company .... 340 people at its two production plants and another fifty at the head office. I normally .... in the production department, but at the moment I .... in R+D, helping them to develop new products. I .... my job because it gives me a chance to travel. At the moment I .... French and German because I have to travel to Europe a lot.

4 Now find suitable verbs in the Present Simple or Present Continuous to complete these gaps:

Let me introduce myself. My name's Jane Slater and I .... for Forest White, a medium sized company which .... paper and packaging materials. I .... my job because it's very varied and I .... lots of opportunities to meet new people.

I .... abroad at least once a month, sometimes more. I'm a sales executive but at the moment I .... in the marketing department. We .... to develop a new marketing policy for southern European markets.

5 Use these auxiliaries to complete this conversation:

'm   are(x3)   is   do   don't(x3)   doesn't

Jill: Hi, Karen.................. you busy?

Karen: No, not particularly. I .... just working on last month's accounts.

Jill: Oh, ... you have to do the accounts every month?

Karen: Well it's not my job really. But Osman .... visiting the Manila branch this week and Paul and I .... filling in for him.

Jill: I see. So you .... get much chance to travel?

Karen: Unfortunately not. I'd like to get away a bit more though.

Jill: Well, why .... you have a word with your boss?

Karen: I did! She .... think I've got enough experience yet.

Jill: That's a pity. Still, I suppose you .... getting lots of experience doing the accounts?

Karen: Yes, but it's the kind of experience I .... want!

▰▰▰*unit 26*▰▰▰
The Simple Past

1 Use the Simple Past of these irregular verbs to complete the sentences:

1. do — In the past we .... more business with the Japanese than now.
2. grow — The company .... very rapidly in its first 12 years.
3. become — We .... a public company in 1985.
4. cut — We .... our advertising budget because of the recession.
5. lend — The bank .... us $45,000 to fund our expansion.
6. get — We .... a big surprise when they made their offer.
7. take — They .... a long time to make up their minds.
8. lose — We .... the contract because of a lower bid.
9. run — Paula .... the company from her home.
10. win — Last month we .... an important order from the Government.
11. meet — I first .... Roberto when we were working in Budapest.
12. make — Last year our Japanese branch .... a small profit for the first time.
13. sell — Greenham Products .... its old headquarters for $46 million.
14. rise — Profits .... due to an improved management strategy.
15. spend — We .... all of our advertising budget in the first six months.
16. fall — Our profits .... last year, but things are looking much healthier now.
17. lead — TransWare, our main competitors, ... the market throughout the 80's.
18. think — Our competitors .... that we were going to increase our prices.

In most of these examples the verb makes a strong word partnership with a following noun, e.g. *do business, cut the budget*. Can you underline the others?

2 Complete these sentences with the following verbs in the Simple Past:

get	**join**	**increase**	**study**	**phone**	**be**	**meet**	**start**

1. The weather .... terrible on Sunday.
2. I .... her at the trade fair in Rotterdam.
3. I .... work at seven o'clock this morning.
4. She .... marketing at business school.
5. I .... the company as a junior manager last December.
6. I .... the 7 am train from London.
7. They .... their prices by over 20% last year.
8. Tina from sales .... when you were out.

3 Now use the sentences in exercise 2 to complete the conversations:

1. So you know Esther?
   >Yes, ...

2. Did you do anything interesting this weekend?
   >Not really. .... , so we didn't go out.

3. Who do you recommend for the new job?
   >I think Julia would be ideal. .... , and she's had a lot of experience.

4. How long have you worked for Lawton's, Maria?
   >Only for a few months. ....

5. You look exhausted, Karen?
   >It's not surprising. ....

6. Are there any messages for me, Christina?
   >Yes, ...

7. You're here early, Bill.
   >... . It only takes an hour and a half.

8. So you don't do much business with Silbert Systems now?
   >No. .... We find the competition much cheaper.

4 Now complete this article from a trade magazine using the Simple Past Tense of the following verbs:

visit	join	help	spend	begin
decide	study	become	leave	complete

We are pleased to announce the appointment of Mrs Maria Teicher as head of quality control. Maria .... chemical engineering at the University of Utrecht and then .... an MBA at Claremont College. After graduating she .... work with ChemTech Supplies in Belgium. She .... assistant production manager in 1989 and she .... to develop ChemTech's Multivit pharmaceutical range. Maria .... the company in 1991 and .... Volcker Foods of California as head of research and development. She .... two years in the United States. Last year she briefly .... our Milan plant and was so impressed that she .... to return to Europe.

5 Now think of a suitable verb in the Simple Past to complete each gap:

This morning I .... work at a quarter to eight. I .... a meeting with my boss at nine o'clock and then I .... to the production plant to sort out an assembly line problem. When I .... back to my office I .... a fax from Sanjay on my desk. He .... me to phone him with details of the Lyon conference. After that I .... half an hour writing the production report. Then it .... time for lunch. I .... Christina in the canteen and she .... me that there .... a lot of problems in her department. She .... me if I could come to a meeting in her office to discuss the situation.

unit 27
The Present Perfect

1 Use the Past Participles of these verbs to complete the sentences:

use   study   meet   see   go   finish   work   be

1. Have you .... Mr Aziz? He's our Head of Sales.
2. How long have you .... for Truman Industrial?
3. So, you've .... to Milan before, Toyo?
4. I can't find my diary. Has anyone .... it?
5. Have you .... this program before, Julia?
6. Elena, have you .... the sales report yet?
7. I think Henri's just .... out for a few minutes.
8. Have you ever .... Japanese?

Now match up these responses:

A   Yes, I was here last year for the Electronics Fair.
B   No, I haven't. I hope it's not too difficult to learn.
C   I think Kristina borrowed it a couple of hours ago.
D   Well, I started to study it but I found it very difficult.
E   No, I don't think we've been introduced.
F   That's OK. I don't mind waiting for him.
G   Yes, I have. Just let me print out a copy for you.
H   Just over ten years. Since I left school.

1		2		3		4		5		6		7		8	

2 Use these phrases to complete the conversation:

have you heard from Tom   **I've been so busy today**
I haven't finished it yet   **have you had a chance to read it yet**
he's left RTX Services   **you've received the Mexico file**

Rashid: Can I speak to Martina, please?
Martina: Speaking.
Rashid: Morning, Martina. This is Rashid from Sales. I'm phoning to check if ....?
Martina: Yes, it's here on my desk. It arrived this morning.
Rashid: Good. .... ?
Martina: I'm afraid not. ....
Rashid: Of course. You're still working on the market survey, aren't you?
Martina: That's right, but .... It's taking much longer than expected.
Rashid: Talking about marketing, ... recently?
Martina: Yes. He phoned me last week. .... you know. He's working for Collinson Investment now.
Rashid: Really? Why did he change jobs?
Martina: I think he just wanted a change.

3 The following adverbs of time are common with the Present Perfect. Use them in these conversations:

since   for   yet   still (x2)   ever   never   just   already

1. Is Mahmoud here?
   >You've .... missed him. He went out a few minutes ago.

2. Tom borrowed my lap-top last week and he .... hasn't returned it.
   >I'm not surprised. He's had my calculator for a month!

3. Have you got those market projections, Daniela?
   >No, I haven't finished them .... They'll be ready tomorrow.

4. Here's a copy of the agenda for the planning meeting.
   >Thanks, but I've .... got one. Julia faxed me a copy this morning.

5. So you've been working here .... six months, Yvette?
   >That's right. I joined the company in March.

6. Have you .... eaten haggis?
   >No, I don't think so. What is it?

7. We've been talking .... ten o'clock this morning and we .... haven't decided.
   >You're right. It's time we had a break.

8. So you've .... been to Canada?
   >No, but I've been to the States a couple of times.

"J.B. has just had this marvellous brainwave – we'll use your idea!"

Study Tip Remember not to use the Present Perfect to talk about specific times:

    *I've got a fax from Pauline yesterday.

    *We've appointed a new sales manager last month.

Use the Past Simple instead.

    I got a fax from Pauline yesterday.

    We appointed a new sales manager last month.

The Present Perfect is used to look back from the present time on a period or event.

The Future: will and (be) going to

1 Underline *will* and *(be) going to* in these sentences:

1. I'll finish them.
2. There are going to be some big changes.
3. I'm going to do a course in business studies.
4. I'll put you through.
5. I'll be there on time.
6. We're going to stay at home this year.
7. We're going to send Raja. He's an expert on the area.
8. I'm going to be a bit late.

2 Now use the sentences from exercise 1 to complete these conversations:

1. Gesteiz Engineering. Can I help you?
    >Yes, I'd like to speak to Ms Johanssen?
    One moment, please ....

2. Don't forget Thursday's project meeting.
    >It's at ten o'clock, isn't it?
    Don't worry ....

3. Sales. Lisa Pavic speaking.
    >Hi, Lisa. This is Alexandra. I'm still at head office. I'm afraid ....

4. So you're going back to college, Mario?
    >Yes, ...

5. I need those figures as soon as possible.
    >Don't worry. .... after I've done this report.

6. Have you seen the consultants' report ?
    >No, but I hear .... at head office.

7. Have you come to any decision about the Dehli Fair?
    >Yes ....

8. Have you made any plans for the holidays?
    >Yes, we've made up our minds at last.
    ....

"Take the lift to the sixth floor, Mr Frensham.
The computer will meet you there."

3 Complete the gaps using *will/(be) going to* and the verb (in brackets):

1. What time's the meeting, Karen?
   >Half past nine. We'd better go or we .... late. (BE)

2. I think we've run out of copying paper.
   >Don't worry. I .... you some when I go out.(GET)

3. So you want to use the computer, Julia?
   >Yes, I .... the quality control report. I only did the first two pages yesterday.(FINISH)

4. Have you decided who's getting the sales job?
   >Not yet. We .... the decision at this afternoon's meeting.(MAKE)

5. Are you ready to order yet, sir?
   >Yes, I think so. I .... the paté followed by the baked salmon. (HAVE)

6. Can I borrow your calculator, Louise?
   > I've stopped lending it - I never get it back!
   Don't worry. I .... it back to you as soon as I've finished.(GIVE)

7. Who are we sending to the Berlin Conference this year?
   >I think Carol should go.
   Good idea. I think she .... a great job.(DO)

8. Have you got those sales figures, Bill?
   >Don't worry. I .... them to you this afternoon.(FAX)

4 Match the situations with what is "going to" happen:

1.	Tina is stuck in a traffic jam.	A	Don't worry, it's going to be replaced.
2.	Elena is looking for a new job.	B	Right, we're going to have an emergency meeting.
3.	Bill's been late once too often.	C	You're going to have to start learning Japanese.
4.	The new computer keeps breaking down.	D	He's going to have a breakdown.
5.	You're being transferred to the Osaka branch.	E	He's going to be sacked if he isn't more careful.
6.	Westgate Construction Plc is losing money.	F	Then, she's going to be late for her appointment.
7.	Rashid works till ten o'clock every night.	G	I suppose she's going to resign, then.
8.	Your main competitors have just cut their prices by 15%.	H	I know the Board is going to call in a firm of consultants.

1		2		3		4		5		6		7		8	

unit 29
Can, could, be able to

1 Use *can, can't, could, couldn't* or *be able to* in the following:

1. I'm afraid I .... help you at the moment. .... you call back later, please?

2. Paul, do you think you'll .... make a meeting in my office tomorrow at eleven? It's quite important.

3. Jane knows quite a few languages. She .... speak French, Italian and German, but she .... write any of them.

4. It looks as if I'm not going to .... go to this year's Marketing Conference. I just .... find the time.

5. Karen, ... I have a word with you? It'll only take a minute.

6. The negotiations with Telfin finally broke down because we .... agree on a price.

7. I'm sorry I .... come to last Monday's training seminar. I had to sort out a problem.

8. I hope I'll .... take my holidays in July this year. If I ...., it'll be my first summer holiday for years.

9. I wanted to start the MBA course in September but I .... because of pressure of work. I might .... start next year, but it all depends on my head of department.

10. Because of better trading conditions, we are pleased to .... offer a 5% higher discount on selected lines for a limited period.

2 Use *can, can't, could, couldn't* with one of the following verbs:
borrow   leave   use   send   help   tell   make   make out   find

1. Telmar Engineering. .... I .... you?
    >Yes, I'd like to speak to Mr Larssen if he's free.

2. She spoke so fast that I .... what she was saying.
    >Why didn't you ask her to repeat it?

3. I'm afraid I .... the meeting this afternoon.
    >Really? What's the problem?

4. .... I .... a message for Mr Aziz?
    >Of course.
    .... you .... him Louise phoned?
    >I'll make sure he gets your message.

5. I left my diary on the desk and now I .... it.
    >Is this it here?
    Yes, I must be going blind!

6. .... I .... the phone?
    >Of course. Just dial '0' and then the number you want.

7. Paula, ... I .... your pen for a second?
    > Certainly! - as long as it's only for a second!

8. I wonder if you .... me details of your model 2650 as soon as possible.

3 Use these expressions to complete the gaps:

Can I get you	**You can't miss it.**
Can I help you?	**I couldn't pick you up**
Could you take a seat.	**I can wait.**
Could you tell me	**we can get started**

Roberto:	Excuse me. .... where the sales department is, please?
Receptionist:	Of course. It's on the first floor, second door on the left. ....
Roberto:	Thank you very much.

Roberto:	Is this the sales department?
Secretary:	Yes, it is. ....?
Roberto:	I'm looking for Mrs Watt. I've got an appointment with her at ten thirty.
Secretary:	...., please. She won't be free for another ten minutes.
Roberto:	That's OK. .... I'm not in a hurry.
Secretary:	.... a cup of coffee?
Roberto:	Thank you. I'd love one if it's no trouble. Black. No sugar.

Lucy:	Nice to see you, Roberto. I'm sorry .... at the airport. I've been so busy this morning.
Roberto:	That's OK. I got a taxi. It didn't take long.
Lucy:	Right. .... straightaway if you like.
Roberto:	Yes, let's do that.

═══*unit 30*═══
Must and Have to

1 **Here are some safety rules from a manufacturing company. Complete the rules with *must* or *must not*:**

1. Safety clothing .... be worn at all times.
2. Cigarettes and matches .... be brought into the production area.
3. Accidents .... be reported to the production supervisor.
4. Machinery .... be operated without safety equipment.
5. Employees .... wear protective glasses while using machinery.
6. Electrical equipment .... be checked at the beginning and end of each shift.
7. Food and drink .... be consumed in the production area at any time.
8. Employees .... run in the production area.

2 **Complete these sentences using the correct form of "have to":**

1. In my last job I .... start work at seven o'clock every morning. Now I .... start till nine o'clock.
2. The computer has broken down again. We'll .... get it fixed.
3. You .... go to the sales meeting tomorrow, Yvette. Isabel can go instead.
4. Karl hates his new job. He .... drive 80 kilometres to and from work every day.
5. I .... go to the production seminar last Saturday. It was cancelled.
6. What time .... you .... be at the airport tomorrow morning, Maria?
7. Don't worry, Tom. You .... stay. I'll answer the phone if anyone calls.
8. How much .... you .... pay for those new printers you ordered last month, Yvonne.?
9. If Thompsons don't offer us a higher discount, we'll .... look for another supplier.
10. I'm afraid Paul .... go out earlier this morning. He won't be back till lunchtime.

3 **Use these expressions to complete the gaps:**

have to make a decision	**have to reduce**
mustn't spend as much	**mustn't do that**
must increase advertising	**must look for**

Lisa: Right. Are there any other ideas before we go on?

Tim: Well, I think we'll .... our prices. Everyone thinks we're too expensive.

Jean: No, we .... ! Extel cut their prices last year, and look what happened to them.

Lisa: I agree with you, Jean. I think we .... other solutions before we start a price war.

Tim: Yes, but we haven't got much time. We .... before the end of this week.

Lisa: In my opinion we .... in the press and on TV. It's the only way to reach new customers.

Tim: Perhaps you're right. But we .... as we did last year. We spent a fortune just on advertising in trade magazines.

4 Remember *must* and *have to* are very similar in meaning.
Mustn't and *don't have to* are very different in meaning.

We use "must" when we are expressing our own feeling:

I must try to give my own opinion in meetings.   (it's important for me)
I must remember to finish those accounts by Friday.   (I feel it's necessary)

We use "have to" to express an obligation coming from someone else:

I have to start work at eight o'clock.   (it's in my contract)
The VAT return has to be in by Friday.   (by law)

Notice the difference in meaning between *mustn't* and *don't have to* :

You mustn't look at those files.   (it's not allowed)
We don't have to show our passports any more.   (it isn't necessary)

5 Use *must, mustn't*, or the correct form of *have to* to complete these conversations:

1. I'm sorry, but you .... smoke in here. Didn't you see the sign?
   >I'm sorry. I didn't notice it.

2. That's OK, Sonya. You .... work on Saturday. The training seminar's been cancelled.
   >Good. That means I can go away for the weekend after all. I .... ring Bill and tell him!

3. We really .... have a meeting some time this week to talk about promotions.
   >Good idea. What about Thursday afternoon?
   Thursday's impossible for me. I .... go to the accountants to finalise the accounts.

4. So Teresa .... travel so much in her new job?
   >No, not any more. She spends most of her time in the office.

5. What happens if I press this red button?
   >You .... touch that! It switches everything off.

6. Why .... Paula .... leave the meeting so early this morning?
   >She .... be at the airport by ten thirty.

7. Let's go. Julia starts her presentation at ten.
   >Yes. We .... be late, must we?

8. You look exhausted, Gina.
   >Yes. I've been working since half past seven this morning.
   You reallly .... try and relax a bit more.

9. When .... we .... settle these invoices?
   > Oh, don't worry. We .... pay them till the end of next month.

10. How many copies do we need of this report?
    > Well, at last year's Board Meeting we .... make 25.

▬▬ *unit 31* ▬▬
Comparing

1 Use these comparative and superlative partnerships to complete the dialogue below:

a much higher salary   **a lot more interesting**

the most experienced   **a much bigger company**

the largest producers   **a lot friendlier**

Frank: So how are you enjoying your new job, Eleni?

Eleni: It's great. Telmer is .... than ALS, so I feel I have a lot more responsibility than before.

Frank: So you find it .... working for Telmer?

Eleni: Well, it's one of .... of telecommunications equipment in the country. I'm working with some of .... people in the industry.

Frank: And what about your new boss?

Eleni   Macgregor? He's .... than I expected. We get on really well.

Frank: And I suppose they pay you .... ?

Eleni: Well, of course, the more responsibility you have, the more you expect to earn!

2 Use the comparative or superlative form of the adjectives (in brackets) to complete the gaps in this letter from a bank.

Scotbank is one of Europe's leading banks. We can offer you a .... (wide) range of banking services than any of our competitors. Our many clients range from the .... (small) family businesses to the .... (large) multinational companies. We have just opened our .... (new) branch in North Street. You will find that we have installed the .... (late) technology to make your banking even .... (easy) and .... (convenient). Our staff is one of the .... (friendly), devoted to making business a pleasure. Don't take our word for it though. Come and see for yourself!

3 Use the comparative or superlative form of these adjectives to complete this description of a hotel.

friendly   quiet   luxurious   wide   good

The Royal Park Hotel is located in one of the city's .... districts, but still only five minutes from the main railway station. Our rooms are even .... than before. With telephone and satellite television in every room, you will not find a .... equipped hotel in town. We now offer a much .... range of business facilities including conference rooms, photocopying and fax. You'll also find our staff .... than at other hotels.

4 Complete the table with the comparative and superlative forms of the expressions:

	COMPARATIVE	SUPERLATIVE
a high salary		
a large company		
high profits		
a fast delivery		
an easy program		
a friendly welcome		
a busy day		
interesting ideas		
uncomfortable chairs		
a difficult problem		

5 Now use expressions from the list in exercise 4 to complete the sentences below:

1. .... we face at the moment is whether to increase investment or not.

2. This time we received a .... than on the last occasion we visited their headquarters. In fact, the last time no-one even said "hello".

3. .... at the conference were put forward by the Italian speaker.

4. With more than 2,500 employees, STC Products is a much .... than most of its competitors in the field.

5. These are .... I've ever sat on. Isn't it time we got some new ones!

6. Shareholders at the AGM were relieved when the chairman announced .... than last year.

7. We use RT Supplies because they guarantee a much .... than the competition. Those insulation units we ordered last Thursday arrived the following morning.

8. The Adword TX2 is one of .... to learn. A complete beginner can use it after a day or two.

9. Huguette earns a much .... than in her old job. She also gets some very generous fringe benefits, like a company car and a housing allowance.

10. Yesterday was .... I've had for a long time. The phone never stopped ringing.

▆▆▆*unit 32*▆▆▆
Some and Any

1 Use the following nouns to complete these situations. When you have finished, underline all the partnerships with *some* and *any*.

experience	information	directions
idea	money	problems
traffic	departments	markets

1. Excuse me. I'd like some .... about your WXP2 range.
   >One moment. I'll see if I can find someone to help you.

2. Frank, could you lend me some .... till the weekend?
   >No problem. How much do you want?

3. The Chinese market is proving really difficult, you know.
   > I know what you mean. Some .... are much more difficult than others.

4. I hope you haven't had any .... with the new printer?
   >No, it's working perfectly for the moment.

5. How long did it take you to drive here?
   >About thirty minutes. There was some .... on the airport road, but not too much.

6. Have you got any .... what time Yvette will be back from headquarters?
   >None, I'm afraid. She went out without saying anything.

7. Did you get lost on your way here?
   >Yes, I did. Julia didn't give me any .... , so I spent ages driving round!

8. So this is your new head office?
   >Yes, most of us have moved in now, but some .... won't move till Christmas.

9. Have you ever had any .... of working in micro-electronics before?
   > Sorry! None whatsoever.

2 Complete the sentences on the left with *some, someone, any, anyone*. Then match them to the replies on the right:

1. More coffee for ....?

2. Has the new sales policy had .... effect?

3. There's .... on the phone for you, Jean.

4. Does .... have any more questions?

5. Is there .... news about tax changes?

6. Could we meet .... time this week?

7. .... called and left this parcel for you.

8. Are there .... direct flights to Algiers on Saturday?

A Oh, good. I think I know what it is.

B That'll be Louise. I'll take it in my office.

C No, nothing's come through yet.

D I'm afraid not. You'll have to fly via Paris.

E Yes, please, but just half a cup.

F Very little! Sales are still falling.

G Yes, why weren't we consulted earlier?

H OK. How about Friday morning at ten thirty?

1		2		3		4		5		6		7		8	

3 Use *some* or *any* plus one of the following words to complete the conversations:

suggestions   **paper**   **German**   **problems**
weekends   **sense**   **replies**   **details**

1. Are there .... you'd like me to clarify before I go on?
   >Yes, there are a couple of points you could go over again.

2. Sorry I'm late. I had .... to sort out at Head Office before I left.
   >Oh, that's alright. It's good you were able to make it.

3. I can't make head nor tail of this fax from Munich.
   >Ask Lydia. I think she knows ....

4. Lydia, can you make .... of this fax in German?
   >Let me have a look. Yes, it's confirmation of the new agreement.

5. Has anyone got .... to make about our marketing strategy for the X310?
   >Yes. I'd like to propose that we target southern Europe first.

6. If you get the job, you'll be expected to work ....
   >What? Including Sundays?

7. Did you advertise the new job in the Financial Gazette?
   >Yes. We've had .... , but not as many as we expected.

8. Did you manage to make those copies of the sales report, Henri?
   >No, I'm afraid not. There wasn't .... left.

*"Someone who loves New York is here to
see you."*

▬ *unit 33* ▬
Quantity

1 Complete these questions with *how much, how many, how long* and *how far*.

1. .... people work in your department?

2. .... time do you spend on the phone each day?

3. .... do you have to travel to work every day?

4. .... does your journey to work usually take?

5. .... languages does your boss know?

6. .... have you worked for your present company?

7. .... is your office from the city centre?

8. .... work do you normally take home at the weekend?

2 Choose the correct alternative in each example:

1. I'm afraid I've had .... work in the past two weeks that I haven't had time to read your report.
   a. too much   b. so much   c. very much   d. much

2. Julia isn't very happy in her new job. She spends .... time away from home.
   a. too many   b. too much   c. many   d. a lot

3. We introduced a "new ideas" scheme last year, but it wasn't very successful. Only .... employees were interested in it.
   a. a little   b. a few   c. little   d. few

4. We were quite optimistic when we launched the RTX4 this time last year. However, ... of our customers were interested.
   a. very few   b. very little   c. very much   d. very many

5. Judy spent four months in Japan but she didn't get .... opportunity to learn the language.
   a. much   b. lots of   c. many   d. few

6. If you give me .... time, I'll check those order details for you.
   a. a few more   b. a little more   c. little more   d. any more

7. I'm afraid we'll have to put our expansion plans on ice for the moment. .... of the banks we've spoken to is willing to lend us the money we need.
   a. some   b. any   c. no   d. none

8. It's company policy to encourage creativity in employees. In fact, ... our senior managers spend one or two hours a day working on their own projects.
   a. much of   b. few of   c. most of   d. none of

9. We need to pay .... attention to after sales service if we are going to expand our market share.
   a. much more   b. many more   c. lot more   d. any more

10 Can I get you .... coffee while you're waiting, Mrs Westman?
   a. much more   b. many more   c. a little more   d. a lot more

3 Use these partnerships to complete the conversations:

very little money	quite a lot of market research
a little more experience	a lot of people
a lot of good work	a few more pages
very much time	a lot of interesting ideas

1. How was the management course, Raman?
   >It was very theoretical. They gave us ...., but I'm not sure how they will work in practice.

2. How was your month at the Chicago branch, Rieko?
   >It was very useful. I feel I've got .... in the information technology field.

3. Hi, Sven. Long time no see! Where've you been?
   > At the Milan conference. Goodness, there were .... there!

4. Can I have a word with you for a moment, Pete?
   >Can you make it quick? I'm afraid I don't have ....

5. Why did you decide not to introduce the TR6 in Italy?
   >Well, we did .... We found that our customers preferred the TR5.

6. Are you sure Eleni's the best person for the job?
   >Quite sure. She's done .... in personnel. It's time she got on.

7. Have you finished the report on the Osaka project yet, Janine?
   >Almost. There are just .... to add on exchange problems.

8. So Jane's enjoying her new job, is she?
   >Well, she loves the travelling, but she's always complaining that she makes ....

4 Complete the sentences using *both*, *either*, or *neither*.

1. We introduced two versions of the HT56, but .... was very successful in the Far East.

2. I'll speak to Karen and Roula to see if .... of them is interested in the trip.

3. We looked at two possible sites for the new factory, but .... of them were too expensive.

4. Would .... of you like something to drink?

5. I'm afraid .... of the departments is interested in the expansion plans.

6. I'm afraid that .... Paul nor Tina came to the meeting on Friday.

7. I've spoken to .... Tom and Sheila, but .... is interested in the project.

8. There are only two possibilities: .... we go ahead immediately or we pull the plug on the whole project.

unit 34
Asking Questions 1

1 Here are 20 common short questions. Add a suitable auxiliary to each:

1. .... we have a break?
2. .... you take sugar?
3. .... he speak Spanish?
4. .... you have a good flight?
5. .... I have a quick word?
6. .... it be convenient?
7. .... you tell me where the loo is?
8. .... you like a coffee?
9. .... you want a coffee?
10. .... we get there in time?
11. .... I ring you back later?
12. .... you hang on a minute?
13. .... you mind holding?
14. .... you been here before?
15. .... we go straight to your hotel?
16. .... they been waiting long?
17. .... you like something to drink?
18. .... it finished yet?
19. .... you like to see the wine list?
20. .... it rained a lot recently?

2 Put these words in the right order to form questions.

1. normally the do weekend at work you

   ....?

2. interesting find your you do job

   ....?

3. company prefer would to another in work you

   ....?

4. in use phone lot your a the job you do

   ....?

5. travel lot do a job you your in

   ....?

6. company branches does have countries your in other

   ....?

7. worked in departments you your have company in different

   ....?

8. people do a you lot employ of

   ....?

3 Here are 8 answers. Match them up with the questions:

> **Yes, I think they will.**
> **Yes, here you are.**
> **Yes, that's right.**
> **No, I haven't got one on me.**

> **Certainly. I'll be here all day.**
> **Not at all. Just go when it suits you.**
> **No, I wouldn't think so.**
> **By all means. It's free.**

1. Can I sit here?

   ....

2. Could I call in for a few minutes?

   ....

3. Do you mind if I leave early?

   ....

4. Have you got a pen I could borrow?

   ....

5. May I borrow your paper?

   ....

6. It was 5.75%, wasn't it?

   ....

7. Is dress formal?

   ....

8. Will they mind if I smoke?

   ....

4 Here are 6 simple questions. First match them to the answers, then match them up with the situations.

1.	Is it off?	A	No, it won't finish for another half hour.
2.	Are you on?	B	Yes, his name is on the list.
3.	Is it up?	C	No, we never switch it off.
4.	Is it over?	D	Yes, our bid was £200,000 below everyone else's.
5.	Is he down?	E	Yes, there were a few seats left in business class.
6.	Were we under?	F	I'm afraid so - a whole per cent - from tomorrow.

i   You were having problems getting a seat on a flight to Hong Kong.
ii   Interest rates are going up from 4% to 5%.
iii   You wonder if the computer should be switched off before you go home.
iv   You are trying to win a contract to build a new hotel.
v   30 people are losing their jobs.
vi   A meeting is taking longer than planned.

1		2		3		4		5		6	

5 One of the most common ways of finding out information - especially in conversation - is to use a question tag. For example:

> **The merger is going ahead, isn't it?**
> **We haven't decided yet, have we?**

Use these tags in the following situations:

did you	**shouldn't we**	**would you**	**aren't they**
can we	**don't you**	**did they**	**won't you**

1. RTL are in the information technology field, ... ?
   >That's right. In fact we bought some software from them last month.
2. We can't really offer any more discount in the current financial climate, ... ?
   >No, but maybe we could offer them better credit terms.
3. So, you'll give me a ring tomorrow with those figures, ... ?
   >Yes, some time before ten o'clock. I promise!
4. You didn't get a chance to speak to Yvette about her trip to Poland, ... ?
   >Yes, I spoke to her this morning. She's calling in some time later today.
5. Nobody rang while I was out, ... ?
   >Yes. There was a call actually. I've left a message on your desk.
6. We should really advertise more in the trade press, ... ?
   >Of course we should. It's probably the cheapest way to broaden our market.
7. You two know each other, ... ?
   Yes, we worked together on the Bormann Schneider contract.
8. Paula, you wouldn't like to do some overtime on Friday, ... ?
   Well, I really wanted to go away this weekend.

Now use the correct tag to complete these questions.

9. Olivier's still working at the Bruges office, ...?
10. We've got at least 25 accounts in Scandinavia, ...?
11. You're going to ask Kate to take over the marketing job, ...?
12. Some of her proposals weren't very practical, ... ?
13. Nobody would mind if I went home early today, ...?
14. This bill includes VAT, ...?
15. We shouldn't worry too much about the safety procedures, ... ?
16. Some of the head office staff have got the week off, ... ?

unit 35
Asking Questions 2

1 Use these question partnerships to complete the questions below. Be careful. There is one extra partnership:

how many employees	whose car	what company
what time	how long	how fast
which subject	which department	whose idea

1. ....did you say it was?
   >Nine thirty. We'd better hurry up or we'll be late for Tim's presentation.

2. .... did Carol use to work in?
   >Accounts, I think. Then she moved to marketing.

3. .... did it take you to reach a decision about the future?
   >Not very long. After we met the consultant, it was only a few days.

4. .... is that over there?
   >The BMW? It's the Managing Director's of course.

5. .... did Sheila study at university?
   >Engineering, I think. She did her business diploma afterwards.

6. .... have accepted the new contract?
   >Very few. I think there could be a strike before the end of the month.

7. .... was it to start a joint venture with Banque Sud?
   It was Lee's idea originally, but we all decided to back him.

8. .... can you deliver these packages to our Denver branch?
   We can get them there by Tuesday.

2 Caroline Jansen is marketing director of the Voorman International Conference Centre. Here are some of the questions she receives from potential customers. Use the question words below to complete the questions.

who	where exactly	which month	how many
why	what kind of	when	how much

Then match the questions to the replies on the right.

1. .... was the centre opened?   A   It all depends on the language.
2. .... is the centre located?   B   It's thirty kilometres south of Gröningen.
3. .... people can the centre take?   C   I look after that area myself.
4. .... extra services can you offer?   D   Because of a huge increase in demand.
5. .... is it necessary to book in advance?   E   Originally in July 1978.
6. .... is your busiest?   F   The summer months. June and July .
7. .... is in charge of conference reservations? G   Up to 500 delegates in our main hall.
8. .... do you charge for interpreting?   H   We provide a full range of secretarial services.

1		2		3		4		5		5		7		8	

3 Use these ideas to write a common question. Then answer them for yourself.

1. How long/you/work/your/company
   ....?
2. Which/department/you/work/in/at the moment
   ....?
3. What/time/you/normally/start/work
   ....?
4. How/you/get to/work/every/day
   ....?
5. When/you/last/have/holiday
   ....?
6. Where/your/company/headquarters
   ....?

4 Use these words to complete the gaps in the article:

director	**rapidly**	**operational**
range	**plans**	**equipment**
factories	**founded**	**present**

Istel Electronics was .... by Paula Schluter in 1978. The company grew
.... and moved to its .... headquarters near Amsterdam in 1975. Istel
employs 3,450 at its headquarters and its three .... in Holland, Belgium and Italy. The
company manufactures a wide .... of electronic components for the car industry as
well as telecommunications .... and household goods. Mr Leo Wouters has been the
group's managing .... for the past five years and has led the company through its
recent phase of expansion. Last month he announced .... to open a new production
centre in Thessaloniki, in northern Greece. This plant will be fully .... in two years'
time and will assemble audio and video equipment.

Now complete the questions about Istel Electronics:

1. When ....?
   >In 1978.
2. Where ....?
   >Near Amsterdam in Holland.
3. How many ....?
   >Almost three and a half thousand.
4. What ....?
   >Mainly electronic components.
5. Who ....?
   >Mr Leo Wouters.
6. How long ....?
   >Five years.

Now write two more questions and answers about the company:

....

....

81

▬▬▬*unit 36*▬▬▬
Prepositions

1 Choose the correct option to complete the sentences. In each case there is only one possible answer.

1. The Marketing Director is away .... holiday. She'll be back .... the end of the month.
   a. in . . in   b. on . . on   c. in . . at   d. on . . at

2. Did you read that article .... the Press about our move .... the Japanese market?
   a. on . . in   b. at . . on   c. in . . into   d. for . . into

3. I need those sales figures .... the end .... the week .... the very latest.
   a. in . . of . . on   b. in . . of . . at   c. by . . of . . at   d. by . . of . . on

4. We hope things will get better .... the second quarter .... the year.
   a. at . . in   b. in . . of   c. on . . in   d. for . . of

5. Will passengers .... flight RT482 please go .... Gate 9 immediately.
   a. in . . on   b. for . . in   c. on . . at   d. for . . to

6. Mr Thomas? He's .... a customer .... the moment.
   a. on . . at   b. at . . with   c. with . . at   d. on . . into

7. You'll find Marketing .... the main building .... the second floor.
   a. in . . on   b. on . . in   c. for . . on   d. in . . at

8. Thank you .... your kind invitation .... attend the opening .... your new retail branch.
   a. for . . to . . of   b for . . at . . of   c. with . . at . . in   d. on . . into . . on

2 Use IN, AT, ON with these expressions of time:

1. .... Thursday
2. 1996
3. .... Tuesday morning
4. .... the summer
5. .... the 1980s
6. .... early September
7. .... the middle of the month
8. .... Easter
9. .... May 16th
10. .... the morning
11. .... the weekend
12. .... Friday night
13. .... the morning
14. .... half past two
15. .... the right time
16. .... winter
17. .... night
18. .... lunchtime
19. .... three o'clock
20. .... the end of July
21. .... Christmas
22. .... a weekly basis
23. .... Thursday June 4
24. .... Easter Monday

3 Here are ten common business word partnerships. Complete them with the correct preposition:

1. ...... the red
2. ...... courier
3. ...... of order
4. just .... time
5. .... trouble
6. .... a trial period
7. .... full
8. .... a lot of pressure
9. .... of stock
10. .... perfect condition

Now use these phrases to complete the following sentences:

11. When the goods left our warehouse they were ....

12. The bank has just rung to say that our no 2 account is still ....

13. Since she took over marketing, Sarah has been................................... .

14. I'm afraid the goods cannot be despatched until payment .... has been received.

15. Don't worry, I'll send you the contract .... You'll have it in two hours.

16. We'll let you have the software .... of two weeks.

17. The photocopier has been .... all day.

18. I thought I was going to be late for Tessa's presentation, but I arrived ....

19. I'm afraid the parts you ordered are temporarily ....

20. The company is losing money fast. They really are ....

"The man we want is the man with the glint in his eye. Are you that man?"

4 **Complete this dialogue with the following prepositions. You will need some of them more than once.**

in   at   by   for   from   to

Alice: So you went from Paris .... Lille .... plane?

Julie: Yes that's right. I was .... a hurry, so I decided to catch a plane and save time.

Alice: Yes, but you didn't think about saving money. Why didn't you go .... train? It's only about 80 kilometres.

Julie: Well, er..., I didn't want to get to my hotel too late.

Alice: Hotel! But you only spent an afternoon .... Lille. Then you caught another plane .... Brussels. And what about this taxi receipt .... 500 francs.

Julie Er..., I went .... the airport .... my hotel .... taxi.

Alice: But 500 francs! Are you sure you didn't go .... helicopter?

Julie: Look, I know it seems expensive, but I did spend two days .... Brussels.

Alice. Yes, staying .... the most expensive hotel................. town according to this bill. You're fired! You've got ten minutes to clear your desk.

unit 37
Writing: Introduction

Business English can be very formal or very informal. This is true of both written and spoken language. It depends who you are speaking or writing to and for what reason. If you are writing a contract, your language will be very formal. If you are replying to a fax from a colleague you know, you will probably write a short note on his fax and fax it back. If you are writing to an American colleague, your language will probably be less formal than if you are writing to a Japanese colleague. Some years ago, there were lots of rules for writing business English. Today the rule is simple – use the language which will best achieve your purpose.

1 Business language can be direct and to the point. At times, however, you may want to be careful – to avoid upsetting a good customer. Re-write the following sentences in more tactful English. At present they are too direct.

1. Your order is going to be two weeks late.
   We regret that there ....

2. We have already waited too long for you to pay.
   Regrettably we must ....

3. You still owe us £2,500.
   There is ....

4. Your invoice is wrong.
   There seems ....

5. We want you to answer this letter immediately.
   We would ....

6. We can't tell you about delivery because we don't know ourselves.
   We are not yet ....

7. We've got none in stock.
   We are ....

8. Please don't go to another supplier.
   We trust that you will ....

"Send someone a bill for a million pounds.
They'll think we've got a computer."

85

2 Louise Thornton is sales director of Reckson Products. What do you think she should do with each of the following communications?

1. Fax it to the Toronto branch.
2. Put it in the wastepaper basket.
3. Enclose it with some sales literature.
4. Reply to it immediately.
5. Circulate it to some colleagues in another department.
6. Pin it on the notice board.

A.   TO ALL MEMBERS OF STAFF

Would anyone interested in forming a staff tennis club please contact Louise Thornton in Sales (ext 347)?

The first meeting will be on Sat June 5.

B.   Dear Customer,

Please find enclosed a copy of our catalogue and updated price list for the spring and summer. You will notice that we have managed to keep most of our prices at the same level as last year and there are even more generous offers of discounts for our regular customers. We look forward to receiving an order from you soon.

Yours sincerely,

Louise Thornton (Sales Director)

C.   Do you need extra money for that new car, the holiday you've been dreaming about or an extension to your home? Don't wait any longer. Get in touch with LoanWise. In a few days we can guarantee you up to £5,000. And we offer you the easiest repayment terms. Anything is possible with LoanWise Finance.

D.   Dear Tom,

This is just to remind you of my Canadian trip next month. I'll be in Montreal on the 14th and 15th and I'll see you in Toronto the following day. Can you arrange hotel accomodation? I'd like to stay at the Fir Tree as usual.

Louise

E   MEMO

To: Roger Martin, Karin Eckstrom, Ulrike Weiss (Marketing)

From: Louise Thornton (Sales)

Alice Rice from Head Office is giving a presentation of the new product range next Friday (7th). I think it would be a good idea for at least one person from Marketing to be there. Is anyone interested in going? Please let me know by Wednesday if you are interested in attending.

F.   Dear Ms Thornton,

I am writing in regard to the order I faxed you last week for 20 x 10-litre containers of Reckson All-Purpose Detergent. We were expecting delivery on Monday. However, it has still not arrived. I have telephoned your office three times and was told that you were not available. Unless I hear from you by tomorrow lunchtime at the latest, I shall have to look for an alternative supplier.

Yours sincerely,

Martine Moreau (Purchasing Department)

3 Look through the extracts in exercise 2 and find suitable word partnerships to complete the following common business sentences:

1. Please .... a copy of our current price list.
2. I look .... to .... your reply by return.
3. If you have any questions, please do not hesitate to .... with me.
4. This is .... you that I shall be arriving around 11am on Tuesday.
5. If you would like me to reserve a place for you, please let .... by Wednesday at the ....
6. If your service does not improve, we will have no option but to look for ....

4 When someone is dictating a letter, it is important for the secretary to record only the words of the letter, not some of the other comments. Can you underline the exact words of the letter in the following:

 Right Jane, letter to Mr D Burke – you remember him, lowest prices, late paying, always complaining, my favourite customer. Dear Mr Burke, should really be cheap Mr Burke. Thank you for your recent letter. I was sorry to hear that you were experiencing difficulties getting spare parts for your XT20. Should have realised if you buy an old model, nobody keeps spares. As you know, this model has been on the market for some time, and yours is the first complaint we have had. Which is not a surprise because most people have better things to do than write the kind of pointless letter which is your speciality.

I suggest you contact Bridge Brothers, who are the importers, direct, as they will be able to give you more up-to-date information than I can on the availability of spares. The address and phone number are as follows, put that in for me would you, Janet, and as soon as we've finished this, let's have a cup of coffee.

I'm sorry I cannot be more helpful – actually, for this clown I wouldn't be – even if I could be – but I am sure Bridges will be able to help. And at last I'll be rid of you. That'll do. Yours sincerely, etc, etc. Put my name but just sign it yourself thanks. Now that coffee . . .

5 Finally, can you make sense of this letter. The writer has had problems with the printer on his wordprocessor and this is his letter of complaint.

Computxr Systxms plc
1Xton Strxxt
Xly

17th Dxcxmbxr

Dxar Sir
Wx rxcxntly purchsxd onx of your nxw modxls – thx 333PCL. I am xxtrxmxly plxasxd with it, but I havx bxxn having problxms with the printxr.
As you can sxx from this lxttxr, xvxry timx you typx an x an x appxars.
As thx printxr is wxll within the guarantxx pxriod, I am surx thxrx will bx no problxm about rxplacing it.
Should I sxnd it back to you dirxct or rxturn it to thx shop whxrx I bought it?
I look forward to your rxply.

Yours sincxrxly

John Milnx

═══════*unit 38*═══════
Dear Customer . . .

1 Use these word partnerships to complete the gaps in the extracts below:

1. I would also appreciate
2. the delay in payment
3. full details
4. Please don't forget to

5. launch date
6. advance copy
7. let me have
8. in the area of

A. Dear Customer

   I am pleased to send you an .... of our latest catalogue which contains .... of the most up-to-date office and information technology equipment on the market. Our "Fast Fax" range is now firmly established with our customers and is available to you at a special discount.

B. I also have a lot of experience .... finance and accounting. Between 1988 and 1993 I worked in the auditing department of Schwartz and Kleinman.

C. Hi Teresa,

   This is just a short note to remind you about Monday's visit from Khalid Assad of the Bahrain Investment Council. .... bring a comprehensive list of our client base in the area.

   Tina

D. I would be grateful if you could send me your current corporate rates for single rooms with bath. .... some more information about your business facilities as I shall be in Brussels for two or three days.

E. Luigi,

   Thanks for leaving a copy of the Chankin Factory proposal on my desk. Unfortunately I can't find page 2 (your analysis of construction costs) and I'd be grateful if you could .... another copy as soon as possible.

   Tom

F. I apologise for .... We have had a number of problems in our accounts department recently and this has meant delays in paying some suppliers. I hope to resolve the problems before the end of the month.

G. Dear Hans,

   Sorry, there was a mistake in the fax I sent you yesterday. The proposed .... for the ColorTex 2XC is now March 16 and not February 16 as I told you yesterday. I'm afraid that there have been one or two technical problems with the main control panel.

   Hope this doesn't cause you too many problems.

   Karen

2

The sentences below come from the replies to the extracts in exercise 1. Match one to each extract:

1. Although we understand the reasons for the delay, we must insist on prompt payment in future.

2. Don't worry. I'll be there on Monday at 2.20. Do you want me to invite Karen as well or shall I come alone?

3. Thanks for telling me about the change of date. I'm sure it won't cause too many problems. I hope the new product will be ready in time for the Warsaw Industrial Fair in the second week of April.

4. Interviews will be held at our Frith Street office on March 15 at 10.30. All candidates should bring copies of degrees and diplomas.

5. Sorry about the missing page. I'd left it lying next to the photocopier. Here is another copy. I hope it makes things much clearer.

6. I enclose an order for 3 HRL FastTrack laser printers and a HRL FastScan scanner.

7. I am sorry to inform you that we have no single rooms available on the dates you specify as there is an Industrial Fair in the city that week.

1		2		3		4		5		6		7	

3

Match the verbs to the noun phrases to make partnerships:

enclose	a 15% discount off list price
correct	a distribution problem
negotiate	a credit account
open	a copy of latest catalogue
resolve	a couple of mistakes

4

When you have completed the following, you will have 8 standard common sentences.

1. We assure you that your order will be .... within 24 hours of ....
2. We would be .... if you could let us have a copy of your invoice no 1066.
3. If ...., we would appreciate it if you sent a copy of the invoice under .... as well as enclosing one with the goods.
4. We .... for any inconvenience which may have been caused as a .... of our oversight.
5. May I say how .... we are at the prospect of our future ....
6. I am a little worried that we .... do not .... to have received the order we placed on January 24th.
7. We agree to your .... and look forward to receiving a copy of the agreement by return.
8. I look .... to hearing .... you as soon as possible.

unit 39
Beginning and Ending

1 Use these words to complete the gaps in the sentences. Then decide if they come from the beginning or end of a letter:

information	enclose	possible	letter
advertisement	wishes	receiving	forward

1. I look .... to meeting you on the 19th.

2. Please get in touch with me as soon as .... if you require more information about the conference.

3. I am writing to you in response to your .... in the latest edition of "Professional Computer".

4. I would also like some more .... about your ScanFast hand-held scanner range, and details of the types of discount you can offer for bulk orders.

5. Thank you for your .... of 12 July.

6. I look forward to .... an order from you soon.

7. Please pass on my very best .... to Stavros and Eleni when you see them.

8. I .... the latest edition of our household goods catalogue and an updated price list.

2 Now choose from the sentences above to complete the gaps in these letters:

1.   Dear Mrs Delroy,

    . . . .

    You will note that our Tuffwash range (on pages 23-25) is now available in four colours. There has been an excellent customer response to the new range.

    . . . .

    Yours sincerely,

    Lois Trent
    Sales Director

2.   Dear Sir/Madam,

    . . . .
    I am particularly interested in your Modex 2 range of colour printers and would appreciate more information about these.

    . . . .
    Yours faithfully,

    JT Sherman

3 **Choose the correct word or partnership to complete each opening to a business letter. In each case there is only one correct answer:**

1. Thank you for your letter of March 24. I am .... hear that our new product has been successful in your market.
   a) please to   b) pleased to   c) pleased for   d) pleasure in

2. I am writing .... your fax of November 12.
   a) to reply to   b) to answer for   c) in reply to   d) in answer for

3. Thank you for your letter of July 17 .... our recent meeting in Hamburg.
   a) reflecting   b) requiring   c) concerning   d) desiring

4. I am .... that you have experienced some problems with our office cleaning service.
   a) delighted to know   b) sorry to hear   c) interested in knowing   d) pleased to say

5. I have just .... your letter of March 11.
   a) supplied   b) received   c) taken   d) had

6. I am writing to .... of our invoice ref. no WLJ42/C which was sent to you on February 12.
   a) remember you   b) recall you   c) forget you   d) remind you

7. We are writing to .... the terms agreed during our meeting of May 16.
   a) confirm   b) contain   c) affirm   d) concern

8. We are writing to you on .... of our customer Mr Spiros Roulis.
   a) part   b) behalf   c) fact   d) condition

4 **Here are some letter endings. All of them contain words which are sometimes confused. Choose the best word to complete each sentence:**

1. If you **require/enquire** further information, please do not hesitate to be in touch.
2. . . . and I am pleased to **include/enclose** a copy of our new product catalogue.
3. Please complete the form and **reply/return** it to us as soon as possible.
4. I promise to give the matter my **soonest/immediate** attention.
5. I am afraid therefore that we cannot offer you a **return/refund** as the goods have already been used.
6. Could you please **pass on/pass off** my very best regards to Mr Mayama?
7. I look forward to **making/doing** further business with you in the near future.
8. I look forward to **knowing/meeting** your colleague Mr Franks at the conference.
9. I hope that half past eleven is **comfortable/convenient** for you.
10. Let me **desire/wish** you the best of luck in your new post.

unit 40
Requests and Replies

1 Use these words to complete the gaps in the letter and reply:

offer	contact	interested	business	writing
enclose	forward	solution	information	

Dear Ms Saregni,

I am .... in reply to your advertisement in this month's "Education World". We are a medium-sized publisher and distributor of educational books and software.

I am particularly .... in your delivery service and would like some more .... about this. I would also like to know if you .... mailing services to the Far East as we do a lot of .... with Japanese firms.

Yours sincerely,

L Kareshi

Distribution and Sales

Dear Mr Kareshi,

Thank you for your enquiry of March 12th. You will see from our sales catalogue which I ...., that EuroExpress has the perfect .... to all your distribution and mailing problems.

One of our local agents will .... you later this week and offer you a free Mail Check.

I look .... to doing business with you.

Yours sincerely,

P Saregni

Director of Marketing

2 In the following sentences there are some mistakes. Underline the mistakes and then correct them:

1. I am writing in reply of your letter of July 5.

   ....

2. I would like some informations about the Datarel 2 software package.

   ....

3. Could you please send me a copy of your actual sales catalogue and price list?

   ....

4. I am send you a copy of our catalogue.

   ....

5. I would also liking details of your discount terms for bulk orders.

   ....

6. I look forward to hear from you.

   ....

7. Please leave me know if these conditions are acceptable to you.

    ....

8. My company has been on the telecommunications business for over 25 years.

    ....

3 First use these words to complete the gaps in the sentences below. Then put sentences 1-6 in the correct order.

well-established   hearing   interest   end   suitable   stand

1. Ms Campert will contact you directly to arrange a .... time for her visit.
2. Thank you for your letter of March 2nd expressing .... in our Greenex range.
3. I look forward to .... from you soon.
4. You may remember that I visited your .... at the Garden Fair in June.
5. My company, as you know, is .... in the United States and Canada.
6. Our export manager, Margo Campert, will be in the United States at the .... of this month.

1		2		3		4		5		6	

The following all need a preposition:

7. We are primarily interested .... your database training program.
8. My company has been .... business .... over twenty years.
9. We normally operate .... a commission basis.
10. Thank you .... your letter .... November 26th.
11. I am writing .... reply .... your letter .... March 12th.
12. And I enclose details .... our Borex product range.

4 The sentences below are too direct and seem rude. Can you change them into more acceptable business language?

1. I want your latest catalogue.
    Could you ....?

2. Give me some information about the forthcoming conference.
    I would ....

3. I want to meet you on June 24.
    Could we ....?

4. I need the cheque before the end of next week.
    Could you ....?

5. Give us details of your discount terms for bulk orders.
    Would you ....?

6. Tell me more about your EasiLux furniture range.
    I would ....?

══ *unit 41* ══
Dealing with Problems

1 Use these partnerships to complete the gaps in the following:

sorry to hear that	**with the situation**
writing to complain	**fully satisfied**
my sincere apologies	**a computer error**

1. Let me offer .... for the delay and assure you that it will not happen again.
2. I am very sorry to learn that you were not .... with our Super Business Class service.
3. Thank you for your letter of April 17. I am .... your order has not been delivered.
4. The mistake in our invoice was caused by ....
5. I am very unhappy .... and would like an explanation from you.
6. I am .... about four ALS Transformers which I ordered recently from your company.

2 Now use four of the sentences from exercise 1 to complete this letter and reply:

Dear Sir/Madam,

....

I placed my order on March 16, and your sales representative, Miss Ling, told me that they would be delivered before the end of the month. We are now in the middle of April and the goods have not arrived.
I have tried to telephone you a number of times, but your secretary said that you were away on a trip.

....

Otherwise, I shall have to look for an alternative supplier.

Yours sincerely,
Khalid Hamid
Managing Director

Dear Mr Hamid,

....

As you may know, the transformers you ordered are produced at our Kunsan plant in Korea. There was a small fire at the factory in February and this caused some loss of production. I am pleased to say that the problem has now been resolved and that the goods you ordered will be sent this week.

....
Your sincerely,

Kim Chan-Lee
Sales Department

3 Put the words in order to form sentences from letters:

1. for apologise the I delay May

   ....

2. very problem to I'm hear delivery sorry the about

   ....

3. happen not that again problem I will this hope

   ....

4. a your mistake There invoice in is number 3749

   ....

5. like offer explanation would I to an

   ....

6. the writing of about complain level to your charges I am

   ....

4 Use these partnerships to complete the letter:

an important customer	a number of problems
for the past two years	another distributor
to complain about	several days late

```
Dear Mr Klein,
I am writing ...................... your Overnite Package Delivery service.
We have been using this service ........................ , and recently we have
had ...................... . Last month, one package of medical supplies
arrived ...................... and the contents had to be destroyed. Because
of this we lost ...................... . On another occasion, a package was
not collected from our warehouse.
I am afraid that unless the quality of the service improves, we will have to
look for ...................... .
Yours sincerely,
R Shastri
Sales and Export Division
```

5 Choose the correct preposition to complete these partnerships:

1. a problem ....delivery   (on, at, with, by)
2. a delay...sending the goods   (on, in, at, with)
3. a complaint...a service   (on, about, in, at)
4. the solution ....the problem   (at, in, to, with)
5. two mistakes ....the invoice   (at, in, to, with)
6. an explanation ....the delay   (at, in, with, for)
7. an apology ....the mistake   (at, in, with, for)
8. a letter ....a missing consignment   (about, for, at, in)
9. a fire ....our main warehouse   (about, for, with, in)
10. a breakdown...the production line   (for, on, at, to)

■■■ *unit 42* ■■■
Another Satisfied Customer

1 Of course business is not only about problems. Many managers receive letters from their customers thanking them for good service. Here are some sentences from thank-you letters. Use these verbs to complete the gaps. Remember to use the correct form of each verb:

pass   resolve   offer   write   thank   accept

1. I am .... to congratulate you on your improved delivery service.
2. This is just a short note to .... you for your contribution to the project.
3. As a non-smoker, I would like to .... you my thanks for introducing a no-smoking policy on long-distance flights.
4. Please .... my thanks for your kindness during my recent visit to your branch.
5. Can I .... on Julia's thanks for all your help during her stay in Canberra.
6. Thanks very much for .... the problem so quickly.

2 Here are 5 common word partnerships from letters to customers. Match up the two halves.

1. deal with
2. express
3. thank you for
4. apologise for
5. send

A.   the delay
B.   my regards to
C.   my appreciation
D.   problems
E.   your hospitality

1		2		3		4		5	

3 Here is a letter to a customer who has written, expressing satisfaction with the service he received on a recent flight. Find one word to complete each gap.

Dear Mr Rahman

Thank you .... your letter of March 25th .... satisfaction with the service you received on your recent flight from Sydney. It is a pleasure to hear from another .... customer. I shall .... on your compliments to the cabin crew. I'm sure they will be pleased to hear how much you .... their hard work.

I notice from our computer that you are not a member of our new Air Points programme for .... flyers in Business Class. This gives you the chance to earn bonus points for .... kilometre you fly with us. It could even mean free flights .... future for you and your family.

I .... an application form and I very much hope you will want to .... this scheme which is already proving popular with business executives like yourself. We look .... to hearing from you in .... course.

In the meantime, I would like to .... you an incentive to respond promptly – a start-up bonus of 500 points and an extra 1000 points if you travel Business Class with us before 31st May this year. That will get you off to a flying start!

Yours sincerely

James Stewart

Public Relations Manager

4 **What is the most important thing for you when you are flying? Mark the following from 1 to 8, starting with the most important.**

A   wide, comfortable seats
B   polite, efficient airline staff
C   good food and drink
D   high standards of safety
E   special offers for regular travellers
F   modern, fast aeroplanes
G   taking off and landing on time
H   special facilities for business travellers

Can you think of any more important points?

"I have your file with me right now, Mr. Brown, and I'm rushing things through as fast as I can."

5 **After a successful business trip it is usual to write and thank your host. Use these partnerships to complete the letters below:**

during my stay   **for your hospitality**
your general manager   **meeting your colleagues**
the end of the month   **do business together**

Dear Mr Fouad,
I am writing to thank you .... during my recent trip to Bahrain. I was very pleased to visit your al-Khadir Production Plant and to meet ...., Mr Abdelatif. I am sure that we will be able to .... in the near future. Thank you again.
Yours sincerely,
F Daniels
Head of Sales

Dear Tina,
Thanks for your all your kindness and help .... in Toronto. I very much enjoyed .... and visiting your wonderful city. I'm sure there are great prospects for us in the Canadian market. I'm reading your market study and I'll get back to you before .... with my conclusions.
Thanks again,
Paul

unit 43
Reading: Introduction

1 What do you read? Tick which of the following you normally read at work?

a daily newspaper	☐	letters and faxes	☐
memos and reports	☐	papers for future meetings	☐
business books	☐	minutes of meetings	☐
travel guides	☐	advertising circulars	☐
software manuals	☐	trade or professional journals	☐
company newsletter	☐	annual report	☐
a monthly business review	☐	legal documents	☐

2 Which category above do you think the following belong to:

1. How to do Business in Korea.
2. Introducing Management Finance
3. Using Windows 3.1
4. The Financial Times
5. Exporters Monthly
6. Draft Contract
7. Heineken Spectrum
8. Scottish and Newcastle 1993

3 Use partnerships from Exercise 1 to complete the gaps in these sentences:

1. You want to know how many shareholders your company has. You can find this information in its ....
2. The Financial Times is the most widely-read .... in the business community.
3. If you want to find out who's been promoted at Head Office in the past month, you should have a look at the ....
4. If you want to know how to print a document using the Adtext 2.4 program, you should consult the .... which came with the package.
5. "African Business" is a .... specifically designed for exporters to Africa.
6. If you want to check up on working hours in Korea you need a .... aimed at the business traveller.

4 Why do you read? Here are four reasons for reading at work:

1. ACTION
2. EXTERNAL INFORMATION
3. PROFESSIONAL
4. INTERNAL INFORMATION

Match these reasons with the following fuller explanations:

A You need to continue learning and studying so that you develop your own thinking and skills.

B You need to know what is going on in your field, but outside your own company.

C You need background information about what is going on within your own company or group.

D You need to do something concrete in the not too distant future after you have read whatever it is you are reading.

Try to decide for yourself how much of your reading falls into these four categories. Can you list them in order of importance for you in your work?

5 Match these business publications to the extracts below:

1. a textbook on modern management
2. a travel guide for businessmen
3. a company's monthly newsletter
4. a computer software manual
5. a company's annual report
6. a leading business daily

1		2		3		4		5		6	

A. This is a relatively expensive city for taxi fares. There is a $5 supplement for trips to and from the airport. These normally cost around $20. Most taxi drivers expect a tip of between 15 and 20% of the fare. Call 032 7755 for a taxi. You will normally only have to wait five or ten minutes.

B. Share prices rose yesterday in London on news of an improvement in the economy. Hillman Properties rose almost 20% on the day to close at 81.5. Manchester-based property group, Stockman Estates, climbed 15% on rumours of a takeover bid.

C. To be an effective manager in today's competitive climate you must keep up-to-date with the latest developments in technology. Technology is changing rapidly and the pace of innovation is accelerating. New technologies are being developed all the time, and this puts even more pressure on managers.

D. With Adtext's Move Forward command you can move quickly through a document. For example, you can go:
* To the top of the following page
* To a particular page number
And, of course, you can also go directly to the end of a document.

E. We are pleased to announce the appointment of Alice Wilson as our new Director of Human Resources. Alice began her career at Smithson Security after leaving University. She has been working at Head Office since last year. Alice is married and has two daughters.

F. Towards the end of the year we saw a slight improvement in our market share in the United States. A more optimistic economic situation there helped our sales to grow by just under 15% in the second half of the year.This was partly due to some very strong competition from other firms.

6 Look through the extracts and find 6 verbs which express a change of some kind:

....

....

7 Match the following to make useful word partnerships from the above extracts:

1. develop
2. announce
3. see
4. keep
5. put
6. begin

A. up-to-date
B. pressure on someone
C. technologies
D. an appointment
E. your career
F. an improvement

1		2		3		4		5		6	

8

The following six sentences were missed out of the 6 extracts in exercise 5. Decide where exactly each sentence belongs.

1. She joined our Westwick branch in 1991.
2. However, sales fell slightly in Canada.
3. Short trips in the city centre are particularly expensive.
4. Of course, this is not always easy for a busy manager.
5. Even to a particular word or phrase in your document.
6. Property shares were particularly in demand.

9

Read the following three business book reviews, then decide who to recommend each to.

Steve - who is going on a sales trip to Poland next month.

Gina - who would like to set up her own business.

Lisa - who is stuck at Ohio airport. Her flight is delayed for five hours.

"When the Chips are Down" by Paul Schuman

Paul Schuman's second novel is set in the tough world of 1980s New York high finance. We follow the progress of Frank Klein, who arrives in the Big Apple in 1979 to join stockbroker Truman Black as an office boy. He rises to control a share portfolio worth over a billion dollars just before the stock market crash of 1987. This is a saga of greed and corruption.

"Eastern Europe, a Business Guide" by Sally Hardacre and Ulrike Reiss

This is the third in Hatchman's "Business Abroad" series and their most useful publication to date. It's a comprehensive guide to doing business in six Eastern European countries. This well-designed book includes everything from how to present your business card to how to order in a Hungarian restaurant. The book contains useful information on leading companies and government agencies. There are also detailed street maps of Eastern Europe's major business cities to help you find your way around.

"Fight to Win" by Katrina Sehm

At the age of 37 Katrina Sehm is one of Europe's top clothing retailers. This fascinating autobiography describes how she set up her first BodyFit Shop with a £5000 bank loan in 1978 and how ten years later she was in charge of a retail group with stores in 18 countries. With the help of top business journalist Julia Tanner, Katrina Sehm shows how determination and ambition can be a recipe for success in today's competitive business climate. A must for everyone interested in retailing.

10

Fill the gaps using words from exercise 9:

1. the stock market _____
2. a _____ clothing retailer
3. a _____ guide
4. in _____ of a retail _____
5. find your way _____
6. a leading _____
7. _____ must for everyone
8. set _____ a business
9. a share _____
10. competitive business _____

unit 44
Difficult Colleagues

1 Match the verbs on the left with the phrases on the right to make partnerships:

1.	to spread	A	on the facts of the case
2.	to create	B	rumours about people in your department
3.	to concentrate	C	three years researching the problem
4.	to spend	D	a good working atmosphere
5.	to make	E	a meeting with your colleagues
6.	to arrange	F	an important decision

2 Now read the text quickly to check if your answers to exercise 1 are correct.

Do you have a problem with difficult people at work? Do you have a colleague who is always late, who is always criticising your work or who can never decide anything? Recent research suggests that you are not alone. Many managers say that they are spending more and more time dealing with difficult people and trying to stop confrontations at work.

Katerina Gerhardt, a leading management consultant, has spent over three years looking into the problem of conficts in the office or on the factory floor. Her report lists some of the commonest types of "difficult" people.

Mr Angry. This person finds it almost impossible to control his emotions at work. If there is a problem at work he becomes aggressive, and shouts and screams until he gets his way. This behaviour can be very intimidating for other people and can lead to serious problems in a department or in a company.

Ms Indecisive. She is completely unable to make a decision. She prefers a wait-and-see approach. Even the most trivial questions take weeks or months to decide. Katerina Gerhardt gives several examples of cases where slow decision making has led to losses of important contracts and millions of dollars in revenue.

Mr Rumour. He is normally an insecure person who feels threatened by colleagues. He may feel that people dislike him or think that his work is poor. His reaction is to talk about people behind their backs and spread rumours about them. This usually creates a bad working atmosphere and can even affect productivity in extreme cases.

Mr Right. He is convinced that his, and only his, opinions are correct and that his decisions are the right ones. Katerina Gerhardt says that Mr Right is very common in senior management positions. He is only interested in himself. He dismisses his colleagues' contributions and will only listen to his own opinions. He is usually the worst kind of team leader.

For some people being difficult is a full time job. This can make life impossible for colleagues and can even lead to people leaving the company.

So what's the solution? Katerina Gerhardt says that some types of behaviour are so difficult that no satisfactory solution can be given. However, she does suggest some ways for managers to deal with problem people.

* First of all arrange a meeting with the difficult person. Make sure that you meet somewhere quiet and not in the middle of a busy office with phones ringing and visitors arriving.

* Listen to his or her opinion. Don't give the impression that you are not interested in the reasons for the problem. Try to find some points you can agree on if possible. Emphasize that you are interested in finding a solution to the problem.

* Don't listen to rumour or opinion. Concentrate on the facts of the case. Turn the conversation to specific cases of "difficult" behaviour. Don't repeat vague accusations or second-hand stories from colleagues in your department.

3 Read the article again and mark the following sentences

T = TRUE   **F = FALSE**

1. In most companies there are some difficult people.
2. Dr Gerhardt studied difficult people in three companies.
3. Mr Angry is usually very relaxed at work.
4. It could be very expensive for a company to employ Ms Indecisive.
5. Mr Right is normally a good listener and a popular boss.
6. Ms Gerhardt thinks that all problems with difficult colleagues can be solved.
7. It is a good idea to invite a difficult colleague to a restaurant to discuss the problem.
8. You should agree with everything the difficult person says.

4 Here are two more descriptions from Dr Gerhardt's report. Use these words to complete the gaps:

watch	**traffic**	**boss**	**excuse**
negative	**complaining**	**position**	**easily**

Ms Complainer. She's often worried about her .... in the company. She hates criticism and tries to avoid this by .... all the time about her colleagues, her ...., and even people outside work. This can have a very .... effect on other people in her department.

Mr Late. You can .... spot Mr Late. He never wears a .... , never knows what time it is and always arrives ten minutes after a meeting has started. He's always got an ...., usually about the .... or a problem at home.

5 Here are some typical comments from the six people described. Who said what?

1. "Have you heard the news about Michel? Someone saw him out with Claire last night."
2. "Er... I think we should. I mean... er. Look, I really need more time to think about this."
3. "I'm really sorry. I was in a meeting with Huguette and it took much longer than I expected."
4. "It's got nothing to do with me. I'm not even in charge of the project. It's all Paul's fault really. If only he'd listened to me!"
5. "Will all of you just be quiet and listen to me for a moment. I'm the head of this department and it's me who decides what happens here."
6. "I'm sick of the lot of you! You're all incompetent! Get lost!"

6 Look back over the text and complete the following with the correct preposition:

1. rumours are spread .... people
2. people work .... the factory floor
3. try to avoid confrontations .... work
4. life can be made impossible .... colleagues
5. interested .... the reasons
6. a bad effect .... other people
7. millions of dollars .... lost revenue
8. don't talk about people .... their backs

══ *unit 45* ══
Managers and Time

1 **Read these instructions, do your calculations on a separate piece of paper, then discuss your result with a colleague, fellow student, or your boss!**

1. Make a note of your annual salary after tax.

2. If relevant, add on any extra bonuses or commission which you regularly expect to receive.

3. Gross your salary up - ie add on tax, employer's contribution, etc.

4. Add on a rough estimate of the expenses your employer pays you, for example, trips abroad, annual cost of your company car, meals etc.

5. When you have a total, decide how many days a year you work, ie not 365. Take off holidays, weekends, public holidays. When you arrive at a number, divide your total costs by it.

6. If you normally work an 8 hour day, divide your daily cost by 8. Remember, if you work 9am to 5pm, that is a 7 hour day, because you have one hour off for lunch - and nobody gets paid for eating! Now you have your hourly rate.

7. When you have found your hourly rate, divide it by 60 and you will discover how much your employer pays you to do one minute's work. Are you shocked?

2 **Now look through the following article quickly and answer this question:**

Why should managers take time management more seriously?

A recent seminar in Budapest on the management of time in business concluded that senior managers are not always using their working time efficiently. Managers know that they can replace old or obsolete equipment and that people who leave a company can be replaced. But lost time can never be replaced. So managers must learn to manage time - their own time and the time of other people in the company - more carefully.

One speaker at the three-day seminar, Dr Jaroslav Lentzer of the Prague-based International Management Forum, claimed that some companies were spending over 40% of time on tasks which were unnecessary or which could be completed in less time. He gave the example of one company in the service sector where office staff spent over half the working day socialising with each other or at "meetings" which had no practical purpose.

"Time", said Dr Lentzer, "is one of the most important resources a manager has. Most companies know what time their workers arrive in the morning and go home at night. But very few companies know how much time their employees spend on useful work."

He told delegates that effective time management must begin with a study of how a manager uses his or her time at the moment. He gave the example of a Canadian bank which issues each manager with a log-book where they record daily activities. Managers are told to write down everything they do during the working day, including apparently trivial tasks like taking phone messages for colleagues. Managers do this for a four week period. Then the completed log-book is sent to a time management consultant who carefully examines the information. This helps the bank to decide how effectively each manager is using his time.

Dr Lentzer thinks that if more companies use this approach they will improve productivity and become more competitive. He says that each manager should answer the following four questions:

* Am I spending enough time on essential tasks?

* How much time do I waste each day on trivial or unnecessary work?

* How much work can I delegate to other people in my department?

* Do I give a specific amount of time to certain tasks - an hour for a meeting, for example - and stick to it?

The next stage is to draw up a "time-plan". Dr Lentzer says that managers should spend at least two weeks on the first stage of the plan. "Make sure your colleagues know about the changes," he says. "And more importantly, make sure they know why the plan is necessary. Remember not to cut out minor but necessary tasks like looking through the business press or talking to colleagues."

Don't let the plan become too restrictive. It should still be flexible enough to allow you to make any changes necessary. Maybe you'll find you need more time to talk to customers or to deal with personnel problems.

3 **Here is the final paragraph from the article. Complete the gaps:**

working day	on the phone	final week	reviewing
once or twice	useful advice	most efficient	spend

The .... of your time-plan, says Dr Lentzer, should be spent ....
the first three weeks and assessing how useful the changes have been. And he has some ....
.... to give to managers. Try to deal with important business at the beginning of your
.... and leave minor things until the end. Encourage colleagues to change their
working habits to make the .... use of their time. Cut down the amount of time you
spend .... Make a note of what you are going to say before you make your call.
.... some time .... a month making sure that your time-plan is working.

4 **Read the first half of the article again and find words with the following meanings:**

1. decided ....   4. aim ....
2. out of date ....   5. workforce ....
3. machinery ....   6. unimportant ....

5 **Find the words in the article to complete these partnerships:**

1. senior ....   6. working ....
2. the three-day ....   7. Prague-...........................
3. office ....   8. effective .... management
4. improve ....   9. the first .... of the plan
5. the business ....   10. .... with problems

6 **Remember the old business saying "Time is Money". Here are some verbs you can use both with TIME and MONEY.**

spend   waste   save   have   make   invest

Use one of the verbs to complete the first gap in the sentence and TIME or MONEY to complete the second one:

1. I think you should .... your .... in the New York stock market. That's the way to get rich!
2. I usually get the train to work. It's a bit more expensive than the bus but it .... me a lot of .... every morning because I get to work much earlier.
3. There are too many meetings in our company. We .... a lot of .... talking about things. But nothing gets done.
4. I'd love to help you but I just don't .... the .... I've got an urgent appointment at head office.
5. Executives at head office have been told to .... less .... on travel and entertainment. All departments have to make economies - from the top down.
6. Teresa enjoys her new job, but she doesn't .... as much .... as she used to when she was on commission.

unit 46
Business Across the Language Gap

1 Read the article and choose the best option(s) to complete each sentence below. Remember that in some cases more than one answer is correct:

Communications today between companies are becoming faster and faster. But there is still one problem that has not been completely resolved: the problem of language. In the United States or Britain, for example, most companies are used to dealing in English. This is fine if you are buying from a German, Indian or Nigerian company. However, when it comes to selling abroad, American and British companies are finding that things are not so simple.

Take the case of a London-based supplier of plastics. Managers were delighted when they landed a multi-million pound contract to supply casings for computers and other electronic equipment to a factory in Iran. Everything went well at first. However, problems began to develop after a few months. The British company had received a large quantity of correspondence in Farsi. But there was no-one in the London office who could read the faxes and letters. So they were sent out to a firm of translators and there was a long delay in replying to them. The Iranian company grew increasingly frustrated at the delays and finally cancelled the contract. It placed its orders instead with a French firm employing a number of Farsi speakers.

Most companies faced with problems like this have little idea of how to set up a language training programme. Some companies then rely on managers' individual efforts. Others hope that secretaries picked up enough French at night school to be able to deal with correspondence.

These responses are not good enough according to a report from the University of London Language in Business Programme (ULLBP). The report suggests that personnel and training managers need to think more carefully about the way they plan language training in a company.

An effective language training programme must begin with an assessment of language needs in a company. One approach is to make a list of the company's main overseas customers and suppliers. This gives a clear idea of which languages are necessary. If your main markets are in South America, then Spanish, and possibly Portuguese, should be high on the agenda.

The next step is to look at the linguistic abilities of employees in a company. A "language awareness test" can help trainers to select those workers who will benefit most from spending time on a new language. A ULLBP study suggests that English speakers who have never studied a language before learn more slowly. They can take three or even four times longer to reach intermediate level in French or German than experienced language learners.

This type of language audit can help a company to plan its training coherently and, in the long run, to make large cost savings.

1. **Most American and British firms**
   a) are happier to deal with English speaking customers.
   b) do not have problems with languages.
   c) may find it difficult to export to some countries.

2. **A British company**
   a) employed a French firm to do its translating.
   b) lost an important contract.
   c) employed several translators.

3. **The University of London Language in Business Programme**
   a) is designed to teach a language in a few months.
   b) helps personnel managers to make decisions.
   c) may save a company money.

4. **Companies need to know which of their employees**
   a) can benefit from a language course.
   b) studied French at school.
   c) have been to night school.

5. **Experienced language learners:**
   a) usually know French and German.
   b) can usually learn a new language more quickly.
   c) should be paid more than other employees.

2 Complete this section from the ULLBP report by putting a partnership in each gap.

proper facilities	**more money**	**language teachers**
language course	**enough time**	**monitor the progress of**

Training managers need to ask themselves a number of questions before implementing a language policy:

- Do staff have .... to study a new language? Should they have time off work to learn?
- How can we .... individual students? Should there be regular tests, for example?
- Do we have the .... for language training? Is there a classroom available? Do we need to buy a video?
- Are .... sufficiently aware of the needs of the business world? How much do they need to know about the activities of our company?
- What type of .... is best for my company? Are modern methods always best or do employees prefer a more traditional approach?
- Can I justify spending .... on language training? Does this represent good value for money?

3 Look back at the article and find the verbs to complete these partnerships:

1. .... in English
2. .... a contract
3. .... up some French
4. .... on managers' efforts
5. .... the case of...
6. .... frustrated
7. .... with correspondence
8. .... language needs

4 Decide which of the following is the best summary of the article:

1. British companies should spend a lot more money on language training.
2. Companies should deal only with companies who speak their language.
3. British people find it difficult to learn foreign languages.
4. Companies who want to export more should pay more attention to their employees' language needs.

═══*unit 47*═══
Travel Expenses

1 These four extracts have been removed from the article. Can you put them back in the correct place?

A   This was over seven per cent of the company's total operating costs.
B   These programmes can help to cut costs.
C   or on inviting their major clients to expensive meals in restaurants.
D   Which trips are essential to promote sales?

How much does your company spend on travel? Even small firms are finding that their travel and entertainment budget can account for between five and six per cent of operating costs. For large multi-national companies the costs can be even higher.

In fact many firms have no clear idea of how much they are spending on sending executives to international conferences (1).

Claudio Rossi, a Milan-based travel consultant, has spent the past year looking at the ways companies deal with their travel expenses. "Very few of the companies I studied could tell me exactly how much they were spending on travel. Only one or two had thought about introducing a system to control expenses."

Mr Rossi gives the example of TransEurop ASP, a Danish transport company. "Everyone I spoke to in the firm assured me that regular trips abroad were a vital part of the work of senior executives. Nobody asked themselves if all this travel was necessary and nobody seemed to know how much it was costing the firm."

In fact when Mr Rossi sat down with TransEurop's chief accountant they found that travel and entertainment costs together came to a staggering $2.2m in a year. (2)

Mr Rossi claims that every medium-sized and large company needs a clear policy on controlling its travel costs. He proposes a four-point plan which companies can introduce over a period of six months to a year.

* Travel expense audit. Begin by asking yourself how the company spends its travel budget at the moment. How much are we spending? How are expense claims processed? (3) Where can we make the biggest cost savings?

* Setting up a policy. Once you have decided how much the company can afford to spend you can begin putting your ideas into action. The plan should involve the company's main travel suppliers - travel agents and airlines - as well as those executives who have to travel most frequently.

* Managing the policy. For larger firms this could mean appointing a full-time travel manager who would be responsible for controlling travel costs and for communicating the policy to other people in the company. This is not a feasible option for most small companies.

* Policy review. From time to time you might need to change your policy to take account of any new offers in the travel market. Many airlines now offer special deals for companies with frequent travellers. (4)

2 **Look at these headlines. Which one do you think goes best with the article?**

Spend More on Travel

Danish Travel Plan

Travel Policy Cuts Costs

Travel Managers to Meet

3 **Mark the following statements about Claudio Rossi T (true) or F (false).**

1. He wants large companies to spend more on travel.
2. He thinks that a lot of companies do not really know how much they spend on travel.
3. He used to work for a Danish firm.
4. He thought that a Danish company was spending too much on travel.
5. He thinks it is almost impossible to control travel costs.
6. His travel plan can be introduced in a few weeks.
7. He believes that people outside the company should be involved in the plan.
8. He feels that all companies should have a travel manager.

4 **Complete these definitions with words or word partnerships from the article.**

1. A company's .... is the money which it plans to spend on meals with customers, trips abroad, visits etc.

2. A .... is a large firm which operates in a number of different countries.

3. A company's .... are its most important customers.

4. An executive who makes .... abroad goes there fairly often.

5. If a company considers a practical alternative, it looks at a ....
....

Now use the same phrases to complete the gaps in each of these sentences:

6. Last year we lost two of our .... to the competition. This year we'll be looking more carefully at our pricing structure.

7. I'm afraid that moving to a new office is not .... for our company. It would cost us far too much money.

8. IBM, BP and Coca-Cola are some of the world's largest ....

9. In my job I have to make .... Next month I'll be visiting Japan, Korea and China.

10. We've had instructions from Head Office to reduce our .... by 20% this year. Senior executives will now have to fly economy class.

═══ *unit 48* ═══
Dressing for Business

1 Which of these sentences are true for your company?

1. Employees are allowed to wear what they like.
2. We are not allowed to wear jeans or T-shirts at work.
3. My colleagues are happier if they can wear what they like.
4. I prefer to dress formally at work.
5. I feel happier at work if I can wear what I like.
6. We are expected to wear formal dress at work.

2 Look at the pictures and label them using the following:

A	a pair of trainers	D	a suit	G	a striped shirt
B	a loud T-shirt	E	a sports jacket	H	an earring
C	a striped tie	F	a bomber jacket	I	a leather jacket

Which of these do you normally wear to work?

3 Read the article and answer the questions which follow.

Simon Harris, a senior executive in the London branch of the computer firm Samex Systems, regularly arrives at work wearing jeans, trainers, and a colourful pullover. His secretary, Martine, is often dressed in a bright yellow T-shirt and designer jeans. Samex Systems recently decided to allow its 1,500 employees to leave their pin-stripe suits and smart frocks in the wardrobe and to wear casual clothes to work.

Samex's Human Resources Director, Norma Leaman is responsible for introducing the new policy. "I travel quite a lot to the USA. Many of the companies I visit there no longer have strict dress codes. In fact, many employees wear practically what they like."

Norma decided to introduce casual dress as an experiment in the company. "We started off by allowing people to dress in a more relaxed way once a week. Then we extended it to two days a week. Now most employees can wear more relaxed dress when they like."

There are, of course, still some rules. Dirty or untidy clothes are not allowed. Male employees are told not to wear earrings at work. And for some people there is still a dress code. Sales staff do not go out on visits wearing jeans. Overseas visitors - especially if they come from the Far East - are not welcomed by executives in Bermuda shorts and beach shirts.

The fashion for casual dress at work started on the west coast of the United States. American hi-tech companies found that younger employees were happier with a less formal style. "In the information technology industry the division between office and home is not very important, " says consultant Luis Rodriguez. "Many people work at home wearing the clothes they feel most relaxed in. When they are in the office, they just don't see the need to dress very formally."Rodriguez has carried out a survey on dress among 700 US companies. "We found that about 70% of companies allowed employees to wear casual clothes on some occasions." There are a number of explanations for the more relaxed modern style, according to Rodriguez. "Companies with a higher proportion of women employees tend to be more relaxed about dress codes."

It is also significant that there are many more younger people in positions of power. "You now find senior managers in their early thirties or even younger. They just don't want to dress like their grandfather did."

Even the most traditional companies have been caught up in the new fashion. Take MFD Securities, a City of London investment firm. For many years executives had to wear white shirts, dark suits, and ties. Now they are allowed to wear more casual jackets and trousers. Jeans, however, are not allowed. "Our customers are getting younger and younger," says MFD spokesperson Jan Martin. "Often they are happier dealing with someone of their own age and background. And that means dressing in a more informal way."

However, not all companies are following the trend. A junior executive in a Paris bank recently arrived at work to find four brand new white shirts on his desk. This was his company's way of saying that blue and yellow striped shirts were not acceptable.

 Answer these questions from the article.

1.   How have Samex changed their dress policy recently?
2.   How was the change introduced?
3.   What rules still exist in Samex?
4.   What were the results of the Rodriguez survey?
5.   Do all City companies have a strict dress code?
6.   What experience did a French executive recently have?

5 Complete these sentences with something from your own experience or company.

1.   You are allowed to wear ....
2.   .... are banned.
3.   .... are acceptable, but .... are unacceptable.
4.   Some people think they should be allowed to wear ....

Answer Key

UNIT 1
Ex 2 1-G 2-H 3-D 4-A 5-B 6-E 7-C 8-F
Ex 3 1 speak 2 leave 3 tell 4 know 5 finish 6 get
Ex 4 1 time 2 busy 3 here 4 meeting 5 department 6 last 7 flight 8 company
Ex 5 1-6 2-3 3-5 4-4 5-8 6-2 7-1 8-7

UNIT 2
Ex 1 1-I Beg   2-I End   3-F Beg   4-F or I End   5-I End   6-F Beg   7-F End   8-F Beg   9 I-Beg
10-F Beg   11-I End   12-F or I Beg
Ex 2 1 Good afternoon, Mr Trent. 2 I'll see you later, then. 3 Hi, Karen. How are you?.......Not too bad.
4 What kind of weekend did you have? 5 Well, I'd better be going..........Thanks for all you help.
Ex 3 Dialogue 1 Hi....fine....weekend....very....enjoy
Dialogue 2 good....Morning....busy....better....later
Ex 4 Dialogue 1   1-B   2-D   3-F   4-C   5-A   6-E
Dialogue 2 1-G   2-C 3-E   4-A   5-D   6-F   7-B

UNIT 3
Ex 1 Conversation 1 met....think....introduce....this....Pleased....heard
Conversation 2 Hello....Pleased....first....before
Ex 2 1 Hello, I'm Tom Wilson. 2 It's good to meet you at last. 3 I don't think we've met before. 4 I'm Tom
Wilson. Please call me Tom. 5 I've heard so much about you. 6 I'd like to welcome you all to our new offices.
Ex 3 Conversation 1   meet....nice....heard....telling....successful....business
Conversation 2 met....visit....couple....colleague
Ex 4 Have you met....I don't think....I'll introduce you....our marketing director....How do you do....Very slowly

UNIT 4
Ex 1 free....introduce....meet.... exactly....software....heard
Ex 2 Lisa works in marketing for BDT where she is Marketing Director.
Louise works for Hilmex as Head of their R & D Department.
Ex 4 1 produce   2 moved   3 flying   4 months   5 involve   6 department 7 call   8 research
Ex 5 1-6   2-3   3-5   4-4   5-8   6-1   7-2   8-7

UNIT 5
Ex 1 Remember to phone Henri in personnel....meeting with Chan Ling from Hong Kong branch....Leslie from
finance department......meeting at Scotbank with Ann Lawson....lunch with Thomas Herber (check restaurant
booking)....phone Theatre Royal (remember to collect tickets)
Ex 2 1-C 2-F 3-A 4-D 5-E 6-B
Ex 3 Good afternoon. Can I help you?.......Yes, I've got an appointment to see Mrs Kerr at half past
two......Could you give me your name, please?......It's Tom Kennedy from Dataplan.......She won't be long, Mr
Kennedy.......That's OK. I don't mind waiting.
Ex 4 see....appointment....sorry....afraid....somebody....waiting... .kind....would
Ex 5 1-P   2-R 3-R   4-P   5-R   6-P   7-R   8-R

UNIT 6
Ex 1 a copy of the agenda......latest developments......International Marketing......remember to bring......give you
a ring......look forward to seeing
Ex 2 Hang on, Louise. I'll just put you through.......Yes, it's sitting here on my desk ......Really? What's the
matter?......I see. How long will it take to repair?......I'll pass on your apologies to the others......I just hope you
get your problem sorted out.
Ex 3 The following are suggestions: 1 I'm very busy.   2 I've got an appointment at the dentist. 3 I was held up
in a traffic jam/I was held up in the traffic. 4 I missed the train.   5 She says her car has broken down.
Ex 4 1 called   2 sends   3 get   4 take   5 discuss 6 have 7 received   8 chair
Ex 5 Other verbs include: hold, chair, miss, interrupt, organise, host, postpone, end, begin, start, finish,
conclude.

UNIT 7

Ex 1 1 Yes. Could I speak to Denise Martin, please? 2 Sorry. Who did you want to speak to? 3 Speaking. 4 "Marsen Electrics"........"Marsen". With an "M" 5 Yes. But I got his answering machine. 6 Just a second. I'll get a pen. 7 Yes, of course. It's Karen Vogel......Certainly. It's V-O-G-E-L. 8 Do you know his extension number?

Ex 2 1 calling F 2 extension G 3 repeating D 4 say H 5 department A 6 fax B 7 back E 8 time C

Ex 3 Conversation 1 Can I.....Could I speak.....put you through......speaking....I'm phoning to check......was just going to

Conversation 2 Can I help you.....This is.....Could I speak to.....I'll just see..... I'm afraid......I'll ring back

UNIT 8

Ex 1 Conversation 1 help....speak....calling....say....spell....put

Conversation 2 speaking....calling....got....have....send....arrived....ring.. ..be

Ex 2 1-R 2-P 3-P 4-R 5-P 6-R 7-P 8-P 9-P 10-R

Ex 3 1 Sorry. Who did you say you wanted to speak to? 2 Could you speak more slowly, please? 3 Which department did you want? 4 I can't hear you. Could you speak up?

Ex 4 1-E 2-G 3-A 4-C 5-F 6-H 7-D 8-B

UNIT 9

Ex 1 1 for calling....is closed....opening hours....on Saturdays....after the tone

2 Sorry I'm not here....leave a message....as soon as I get back

Ex 2 1 ask....ring....that's....repeat....fax

2 trying....machine....urgently....check....possible

Ex 3 1-D 2-A 3-E 4-B 5-F 6-C

Ex 4 1 as soon as possible......urgent 2 departure......ETA 3 out of stock...... temporary 4 apologies

UNIT 10

Ex 1 Introducing: Would you like to join us? Inviting: I don't have anything planned.......Fine. That'll give me time to get changed. Refusing: Some other time, maybe? Suggesting: Let me show you some of the sights......Do you fancy a quick jog round the block?

Ex 2 hope....join....meeting....give....make....see

Ex 3 1-C 2-F 3-G 4-K 5-A 6-H 7-D 8-L 9-I 10-E 11-B 12-J

UNIT 11

Ex 1 work for.....the personnel department......in sales.....to deal with problems.....on an everyday basis......a good working atmosphere......we all know each other......it gives me the opportunity to......a training conference

Ex 2 1 deal with 2 get on 3 the opportunity to travel 4 at the moment 5 a chance...... meet people

Ex 4 1 direct flight 2 travel agent 3 economy class 4 business trip 5 jet lag 6 travel expenses

Ex 5 Here are the partnerships: sales costs, sales problems, sales manager, sales department, sales consultants; transport costs, transport problems, transport manager, transport department, transport consultant; bank costs, bank problems, bank manager; management costs, management problems, management department, management consultants; production costs, production problems, production manager, production department, production line, production consultants; software costs, software problems, software consultants.

1 bank manager 2 software consultants 3 transport problems 4 management consultant 5 production line

Ex 6 The verbs which do not form partnerships are: 1 work deal 2 copy send 3 return post 4 send get 5 deal buy 6 hold deal

Ex 7 1-AB 2-A 3-BC 4-CD 5-AB 6-ACD 7-BC 8-C 9-BD 10-ABCD

UNIT 12

Ex 1 1 stapler 2 diskette 3 calendar 4 scissors 5 paper clip 6 note pad 7 calculator 8 desk diary 9 drawer 10 rubber stamp 11 folder 12 envelope

Ex 2 1 borrow your calculator 2 pass me my diary 3 for this envelope......in the bottom drawer 4 a pair of scissors 5 blank diskettes

Ex 3 1-E 2-G 3-A 4-B 5-H 6-C 7-D 8-F

Ex 4 1 post a couple of letters 2 order some photocopy paper 3 answer the phone 4 book a hotel room 5 repair the printer 6 check the sales figures

Ex 5 1 need....leave 2 know....give 3 get....meet 4 make....let 5 do....lend 6 have....return

UNIT 13

Ex 1 1-H 2-E 3-I 4-F 5-G 6-A 7-B 8-C 9-J 10-D

Ex 3 The words which do not form partnerships are: 1 ask, meet 2 work, market 3 meet, ask 4 give, make

Ex 4 1 responsible....consumers....launching....questionnaires (marketing) 2 biggest....shifts....technical....supervise (production) 3 check....maintain.... standards (quality control)
4 scientific....background....improving (research and development) 5 recruiting....sacking (personnel)

UNIT 14

Ex 1 The following are examples of partnerships: the leading Danish pharmaceuticals group......announce plans....rapidly expanding....a leading management consultant.....state sector enterprises.....productivity bonuses.....hold an inquiry into allegations.....one of the country's top manufacturing companies.....breach import regulations.....Hamburg-based......announce plans....loss-making....fail to reach an agreement.

Ex 2 1 pharmaceutical company 2 highly profitable 3 biggest employers 4 chemicals division
5 food distribution groups 6 family run 7 Florida-based 8 loss-making manufacturer

Ex 3 fairly diversified......two main divisions......on the publishing side......about 500 people......directly under......in the pipeline

Ex 4 Name of Company: Micropol AT   Activities: producing software   Workforce: over 1,000 employees   Location: Santa Monica   Turnover: $300 million   Profits: highly profitable Market: industry and education   Plans: to launch a new program and form a joint venture

Ex 5 was founded.....main products......Company President......ambitious plans......on the market......joint venture

UNIT 15

Ex 1 1-C 2-D 3-E 4-B 5-A 6-J 7-H 8-F 9G 10-I

Ex 2 1 time difference 2 expense claim 3 travel agents......business class 4 boarding card......hand luggage
5 duty free 6 taxi fare

Ex 3 The verbs which do not fit are as follows: 1 travel, fly 2 catch, run 3 travel, catch 4 miss, catch

Ex 4 1 confirm 2 check in 3 hire 4 change 5 meet 6 miss 7 stay 8 land

Ex 5 1-B 2-A 3-C 4-B 5-B 6-C 7-C 8-A

UNIT 16

Ex 1 1 high-quality G 2 small enough C 3 fast-changing F 4 with ice D 5 latest technology A
6 hard-wearing H 7 short-sleeved E 8 remote control B

Ex 2 1 discount 2 price 3 information 4 cost 5 deliver 6 models 7 market 8 available

Ex 3 6 7 8 4 1 2 5 3

Ex 4 1 It's not very user-friendly. 2 It's not very cheap. 3 Yes. It's not very good. 4 You're right. They're not very efficient. 5 Yes. They're not very polite. 6 You're right. They're not very profitable.

Ex 5 1 rude, expanding 2 friendly, strong 3 heavy, user-friendly 4 product, sure

UNIT 17

Ex 1 FISH: salmon haddock cod trout herring
SEAFOOD: scampi lobster octopus prawns crab mussels squid
MEAT: lamb steak beef ham pork veal
POULTRY: chicken turkey duck pheasant
VEGETABLES: potatoes broccoli cabbage onions tomatoes brussels sprouts spinach carrots
FRUIT: peaches apples pears oranges grapes plums

Ex 2 1 a light meal 2 stale bread 3 mild food 4 sparkling water 5 dry wine 6 cold soup 7 an alcoholic drink 8 a well-done steak

Ex 3 1 book 2 suit 3 order 4 recommend 5 start....follow 6 prefer 7 eat 8 have 9 ask 10 bring....take

Ex 4 1 have 2 find 3 fancy 4 try 5 eat 6 love 7 get 8 take

Ex 5 Do you fancy something to eat?......Let's try the Taj Mahal for a change......I find curry too spicy......I love Mediterranean food......I eat there fairly often......How long will it take?......Can I get you something to drink?......I'll have a mineral water, please.

Ex 6 menu....recommend....starter....sounds....order....follow....seafood.....bill....pay....wonderful

UNIT 18

Ex 1 1 keep up 2 lend 3 earns 4 save 5 spent 6 losing 7 taken out....owe 8 make....invest

Ex 2 1 open 2 change 3 cash 4 pay 5 make 6 use 7 change two hundred dollars 8 cash this cheque
9 open a current account 10 pay bank charges 11 use the cash dispenser 12 make a bank transfer

Ex 3 branch....location....services....financial....range....interest ....staff....currency....charges....fortnightly

Ex 4 borrow some money......moved my account......some more information......in business......profit and loss account......cash flow forecast

UNIT 19

Ex 1 1-F 2-K 3-A 4-H 5-C 6-E 7-N 8-P 9-B 10-G 11-J 12-L 13-D 14-O 15-M 16-I

Ex 3 1-T 2-F 3-T 4-F 5-T 6-F 7-T 8-F 9-T 10-F

Ex 4 1 three thousand four hundred and fifty six 2 twenty three point six four percent 3 two and a half
4 one and three quarters 5 twenty seven square metres 6 three feet by five feet

UNIT 20

Ex 1 1 get to the office 2 get a headache 3 get that last point 4 get me a copy 5 get the fax 6 get used to it
7 get a taxi 8 got any idea

Ex 2 1-C 2-E 3-F 4-B 5-D 6-A

Ex 3 Possible answers are: a cold, lost, caught, the bus, the plane, the train, the ferry, the only one left, the paper, a present, the contract, it fixed etc.

Ex 4 A get a chance B get home C get a pay rise D get over $50,000 E get married F get someone a coffee
G get someone a present H get a phone call I get a direct flight J get started

Ex 5 1-F 2-G 3-J 4-A 5-D 6-H 7-B 8-I 9-C 10-E

UNIT 21

Ex 1 1 make....do 2 do 3 made 4 do 5 making 6 do 7 make 8 made 9 do 10 done

Ex 2 1 make a call 2 make sure 3 making much progress 4 do my best 5 doing the figures 6 do without

Ex 3 1 doing 2 made 3 made 4 done 5 make 6 making 7 do 8 do 9 did 10 make

Ex 4 1 May I make a suggestion? 2 Could you do me a favour? 3 What are you doing this weekend? 4 She's gone to Paris to do a computing course. 5 I think you've made a mistake here. 6 We did some market research last year 7 Have you done those sales figures yet, Michel? 8 No, I'd rather make a start right away.

UNIT 22

Ex 1 The partnerships (in brackets) are suggestions only: 1 manage manager management (departmental manager) 2 sell salesman sales/selling (sales figures) 3 advertise advertiser advertising (advertising agency)
4 buy buyer buying (the head buyer) 5 consult consultant consultation/consulting (a management consultant)
6 train trainer/trainee training (a trainee manager) 7 present presenter presentation (present a report) 8 assist assistant assistance (a managerial assistant) 9 employ employer/employee employment (an equal opportunity employer) 10 operate operator operation (operate a system)   11 advise adviser advice (sound advice)
12 consume consumer consumption (consumer protection legislation) 13 deal dealer dealing/deal (a second-hand car dealer) 14 produce producer production/producing (NB farm produce where produce is a noun)

Ex 2 1 advise 2 managers/management 3 advertising 4 training 5 consumers 6 buyer 7 deal
8 products.......production

Ex 3 1 consultants 2 sales 3 advertising 4 adviser 5 management 6 assistant 7 speech 8 operator
9 employers.....employees 10 dealers

Ex 4 1 a) appointment b) appointed   2 a) organisation b) disorganised   3 a) introductory b) introduction
4 a) Development b) developers   5 a) producer b) produce c) production

UNIT 23

Ex 1 1-G 2-D 3-A 4-J 5-F 6-I 7-E 8-B 9-H 10-C

Ex 2 1-B 2-C 3-F 4-G 5-H 6-A 7-D 8-E

Ex 3 1 verb 2 adjective 3 adjective 4 noun 5 verb 6 verb 7 noun 8 verb 9 verb 10 adjective

Ex 5 1 So I'll see you on Monday, then? 2 What does this word here mean? 3 She works in the personnel department now. 4 Could I speak to the sales manager, please? 5 It's the biggest software producer in the country. 6 Who wrote this report? 7 Were there many people at the telecommunications conference?
8 ... but none of our customers was interested.

UNIT 24

Ex 1 1 an accountant....a medium-sized....the most important....the country....a wide range....the automobile industry....the only thing....the weekend.

2 a fax....a meeting....the next two months....a ring....a time.

3 a marketing conference....the conference....a beautiful location....an excellent opportunity....the current state....a firm decision....the latest.

4 the Claymore....a luxury hotel....a comfortable....a fax machine....an important document.....a pool....an important meeting....a luxury boardroom....the Claymore....a ring.

5 a recent study....the highest paid....the report....the Simon Hartner Consultancy....the top earners....the figures.

Ex 2 1 a finance house   2 a parking space   3 a shopping centre   4 an instruction manual   5 an information desk   6 a cash dispenser   7 an advice column   8 a traffic jam

Ex 3 1 a traffic jam   2 an advice column   3 a parking space   4 a shopping centre   5 an information desk 6 a cash dispenser   7 an instruction manual   8 a finance house

UNIT 25

Ex 1 A-C   B-S   C-S   D-S   E-C   F-S   G-C   H-C

Ex 2 1 I go abroad at least once a month.   2 Which other languages do you speak, Sven?   3 I'm getting used to it.   4 I'm still waiting for a call from head office.   5 We provide catering and cleaning for big companies. 6 What are you planning to do in the holidays, Tom?   7 I'm trying to get through to Rashid Aziz in Accounts. 8 How long does it take to deliver to Manchester?

Ex 3 live....manufactures....employs....work....am working....enjoy....am studying

Ex 4 work....makes/produces....enjoy/like....get....go/travel....am working....are trying

Ex 5 are....'m....do....is....are....don't....don't....doesn't....are....don't

UNIT 26

Ex 1 1 did   2 grew   3 became   4 cut   5 lent   6 got   7 took   8 lost   9 ran   10 won   11 met   12 made 13 sold   14 rose   15 spent   16 fell   17 led   18 thought

Ex 2 1 was 2 met 3 started 4 studied 5 joined 6 got 7 increased 8 phoned

Ex 3 1-2   2-1   3-4   4-5   5-3   6-8   7-6   8-7

Ex 4 studied....completed....began....became....helped....left....joined....spent....visited....decided

Ex 5 started/began....had....went....got....found....asked....spent. ...was....met....told.... were....asked

UNIT 27

Ex 1 1 met (E)   2 worked (H)   3 been (A)   4 seen (C)   5 used (B)   6 finished (G)   7 gone (F)   8 studied (D)

Ex 2 you've received the Mexico file......have you had a chance to read it yet.......I've been so busy today.......I haven't finished it yet.......have you heard from Tom......he's left RTX Services

Ex 3 1 just   2 still   3 yet   4 already   5 for   6 ever   7 since....still   8 never

UNIT 28

Ex 1 1 'll finish   2 are going to be   3 'm going to do   4 'll put   5 'll be   6 're going to stay   7 're going to send 8 'm going to be

Ex 2 1 I'll put you through.   2 I'll be there on time.   3 I'm going to be a bit late.   4 I'm going to do a course in business studies.   5 I'll finish them.   6 There are going to be some big changes. 7 We're going to send Raja. He's an expert on the area. 8 We're going to stay at home this year.

Ex 3 1 we're going to be late/we'll be late   2 I'll get you some   3 I'm going to finish   4 We're going to make the decision   5 I'll have the pate   6 I'll give it back to you   7 she'll do a great job   8 I'll fax them to you

Ex 4 1-F   2-G   3-E   4-A   5-C   6-H   7-D   8-B

UNIT 29

Ex 1 1 can't....Could   2 be able to   3 can....can't   4 be able to....can't   5 can   6 couldn't   7 couldn't   8 be able to....can   9 couldn't....be able to   10 be able to

Ex 2 1 Can I help you? 2 I couldn't make out   3 I can't make the meeting 4 Could I leave a message?......Could you tell him   5 I can't find it   6 Can I use the phone?   7 can I borrow your pen? 8 I wonder if you could send me details

Ex 3 Could you tell me.......You can't miss it......Can I help you......Could you take a seat......I can wait......Can I get you......I couldn't pick you up......we can get started

UNIT 30

Ex 1 1 must 2 must not 3 must 4 must not 5 must 6 must 7 must not 8 must not
Ex 2 1 had to......don't have to 2 have to 3 don't have to 4 has to 5 didn't have to 6 do you have to
7 don't have to 8 did you have to 9 have to 10 had to
Ex 3 have to reduce......mustn't do that......must look for......have to make a decision......must increase
advertising......mustn't spend as much
Ex 5 1 mustn't 2 don't have to......must 3 must......have to 4 doesn't have to 5 mustn't 6 did Paula have
to......had to 7 mustn't 8 must 9 do we have to......don't have to 10 had to

UNIT 31

Ex 1 a much bigger company......a lot more interesting......the largest producers......the most experienced......a
lot friendlier......a much higher salary
Ex 2 wider......smallest......largest......newest......latest......easier......more convenient......friendliest
Ex 3 quietest.....more luxurious......better......wider......friendlier
Ex 4 a higher salary the highest salary; a larger company the largest company; higher profits the highest
profits; a faster delivery the fastest delivery; an easier program the easiest program; a friendlier welcome the
friendliest welcome; a busier day the busiest day; more interesting ideas the most interesting ideas; more
uncomfortable chairs the most uncomfortable chairs; a more difficult problem the most difficult problem
Ex 5 1 the most difficult problem 2 friendlier welcome 3 the most interesting ideas 4 larger company
5 the most uncomfortable chairs 6 higher profits 7 faster delivery 8 the easiest programs 9 higher salary
10 the busiest day

UNIT 32

Ex 1 1 information 2 money 3 markets 4 problems 5 traffic 6 idea 7 directions 8 departments
9 experience
Ex 2 1 anyone (E) 2 any (F) 3 someone (B) 4 anyone (G) 5 any (C) 6 some (H) 7 someone (A)
8 any (D)
Ex 3 1 any details 2 some problems 3 some German 4 any sense 5 any suggestions 6 some weekends
7 some replies 8 any paper

UNIT 33

Ex 1 1 how many 2 how much 3 how far 4 how long 5 how many 6 how long 7 how far 8 how much
Ex 2 1-B 2-B 3-B 4-A 5-A 6-B 7-D 8-C 9-A 10-C
Ex 3 1 a lot of interesting ideas 2 a little more experience 3 a lot of people 4 very much time 5 quite a lot of
market research 6 a lot of good work 7 a few more pages 8 very little money
Ex 4 1 neither 2 either 3 both 4 either 5 neither 6 neither 7 both....neither 8 either

UNIT 34

Ex 1 1 can/shall 2 do 3 does/can 4 did 5 can/could/may 6 would 7 can/could 8 would 9 do 10 can
11 could/can 12 could/can 13 would 14 have 15 shall 16 have 17 would 18 is 19 would 20 has
Ex 2 1 Do you normally work at the weekend? 2 Do you find your job interesting? 3 Would you prefer to
work in another company? 4 Do you use the phone a lot in your job? 5 Do you travel a lot in your job?
6 Does your company have branches in other countries? 7 Have you worked in different departments in your
company? 8 Do you employ a lot of people?
Ex 3 1 By all means. It's free. 2 Certainly. I'll be here all day. 3 Not at all. Just go when it suits you.
4 No, I haven't got one on me. 5 Yes, here you are. 6 Yes, that's right. 7 No, I wouldn't think so.
8 Yes, I think they will.
Ex 4 1-C (iii) 2-E (i) 3-F (ii) 4-A (vi) 5-B (v) 6-D (iv)
Ex 5 1 aren't they 2 can we 3 won't you 4 did you 5 did they 6 shouldn't we 7 don't you 8 would you
9 isn't he 10 haven't we 11 aren't you 12 were they 13 would they 14 doesn't it 15 should we 16 haven't
they

UNIT 35

Ex 1 1 what time 2 which department 3 how long 4 whose car 5 which subject 6 how many employees
7 whose idea 8 how fast
Ex 2 1 when (E) 2 where exactly (B) 3 how many (G) 4 what kind of (H) 5 why (D) 6 which month (F)
7 who (C) 8 how much (A)
Ex 3 1 How long have you worked for your company? 2 Which department are you working in at the

moment?　3 What time do you normally start work?　4 How do you get to work every day?　5 When did you last have a holiday?　6 Where are your company headquarters?

Ex 4 founded......rapidly......present......factories......range.....equipment......director.....plans......operational

1 When was the company founded?　2 Where are the company headquarters?　3 How many people does Istel Electronics employ?　4 What does the company manufacture?　5 Who is the company's managing director? 6 How long has he been managing director?

Other possible questions: Who founded Istel? (Paula Schluter) When did the company move? (in 1978) Where are the three factories? (Holland, Belgium, and Italy) Where will the fourth factory be? (Thessaloniki in Greece) How long will it take for it to be fully operational? (Two years) What will that factory produce? (audio and video equipment)

UNIT 36

Ex 1 1-D　2-C　3-C　4-B　5-D　6-C　7-A　8-A

Ex 2 1 on　2 in　3 on　4 in　5 in　6 in　7 in　8 at　9 on　10 in　11 at　12 on　13 in　14 at　15 at　16 in 17 at　18 at　19 at　20 at　21 at　22 on　23 on　24 on

Ex 3 1 in　2 by　3 out　4 in　5 in　6 for　7 in　8 under 9 out　10 in　11 in perfect condition　12 in the red 13 under a lot of pressure　14 in full　15 by courier　16 for a trial period　17 out of order 18 just in time 19 out of stock　20 in trouble

Ex 4 to Lille by plane......in a hurry.....by train......in Lille.....to Brussels....for 500 francs.....from the airport to my hotel by taxi....by helicopter.....in Brussels....at the most expensive hotel in town

UNIT 37

Ex 1 1 We regret that there is going to be a two week delay in supplying your order.　2 Regrettably we must insist on immediate payment.　3 There is still £2,500 outstanding.　4 There seems to be a mistake in your invoice. 5 We would appreciate an immediate answer. (or an answer by return)　6 We are not yet in a position to give you a firm delivery date.　7 We regret we are temporarily out of stock of that particular item.　8 We trust that you will not look elsewhere. (look for an alternative supplier)

Ex 2 1-D　2-C　3-B　4-F　5-E　6-A

Ex 3 1 find enclosed　2 forward to receiving　3 get in touch　4 just to remind　5 let me know.......at the latest 6 another supplier

Ex 4 Dear Mr Burke,

Thank you for your recent letter. I was sorry to hear that you were experiencing difficulties getting spare parts for your XT20. As you know, this model has been on the market for some time, and yours is the first complaint we have had. I suggest you contact Bridge Brothers, who are the importers, direct, as they will be able to give you more up-to-date information than I can on the availability of spares. The address and phone number are as follows........ . I'm sorry I cannot be more helpful, but I am sure Bridges will be able to help.

Yours sincerely

pp (name of writer)

Ex 5 Computersystems, 1 Eton Street, Ely. 17th December.

Dear Sir,

We recently purchased one of your new models - the 333PCL. I am extremely pleased with it, but I have been having problems with the printer.

As you can see from this letter, every time you type an e an x appears.

As the printer is well within the guarantee period, I am sure there will be no problems about replacing it. Should I send it back to you direct or return it to the shop where I bought it?

I look forward to your reply.

Yours sincerely

John Milne

UNIT 38

Ex 1 A-6,3　B-8　C-4　D-1　E-7　F-2　G-5

Ex 2 1-F　2-C　3-G　4-B　5-E　6-A　7-D

Ex 3 enclose a copy of latest catalogue......correct a couple of mistakes......negotiate a 15% discount off list price.....open a credit account.....resolve a distribution problem

Ex 4 1 dispatched within 24 hours of receipt　2 grateful　3 possible........separate cover 4 apologise.......result　5 delighted/please........cooperation　6 we still do not seem to have received 7 proposal/suggestion　8 I look forward to hearing from you

UNIT 39

Ex 1 1 forward (E) 2 possible (E) 3 advertisement (B) 4 information (E) 5 letter (B) 6 receiving (E) 7 wishes (E) 8 enclose (B)

Ex 2 1-8....6 2-3....4

Ex 3 1-B 2-C 3-C 4-B 5-B 6-D 7-A 8-B

Ex 4 1 require 2 enclose 3 return 4 immediate 5 refund 6 pass on 7 doing 8 meeting 9 convenient 10 wish

UNIT 40

Ex 1 First letter: writing......interested......information......offer.....business
Second letter: enclose......solution.....contact.....forward

Ex 2 1 I am writing in reply to 2 I would like some information 3 Could you please send me a copy of your current sales catalogue and price list? 4 I am sending you a copy 5 I would also like details 6 I look forward to hearing from you 7 Please let me know 8 My company has been in the telecommunications business

Ex 3 1 suitable 2 interest 3 hearing 4 stand 5 well-established 6 end 7 in 8 in....for 9 on 10 for....of 11 in....to....of 12 of
The correct order of nos 1-6 is: 2-4-5-6-1-3

Ex 4 1 Could you send me a copy of your latest catalogue? 2 I would like some information about the forthcoming conference. 3 Could we meet on June 24? 4 Could you send us the cheque before the end of the week? 5 Would you please give us details of your discount terms for bulk orders? 6 I would appreciate some more information about your Easilux furniture range?

UNIT 41

Ex 1 1 my sincere apologies 2 fully satisfied 3 sorry to hear that 4 a computer error 5 with the situation 6 writing to complain

Ex 2 First letter: 6........5 Second letter: 3......1

Ex 3 1 May I apologise for the delay? 2 I'm very sorry to hear about the delivery problem. 3 I hope that this problem will not happen again.
4 There is a mistake in your invoice no 3749. 5 I would like to offer an explanation. 6 I am writing to complain about the level of your charges.

Ex 4 1 to complain about......for the past two years......a number of problems...... several days late......an important customer......another distributor

Ex 5 1 with 2 in 3 about 4 to 5 in 6 for 7 for 8 about 9 in 10 on

UNIT 42

Ex 1 1 writing 2 thank 3 offer 4 accept 5 pass 6 resolving

Ex 2 1-D 2-C 3-E 4-A 5-B

Ex 3 for....expressing......satisfied......pass.....appreciated..... frequent......every......in enclose......join......forward.....due....offer

Ex 5 for your hospitality......your general manager......do business together......during my stay......meeting your colleagues......the end of the month

UNIT 43

Ex 2 1 travel guides 2 business books 3 software manuals 4 a daily newspaper 5 trade or professional journals 6 papers for future meetings 7 a company newsletter 8 an annual report

Ex 3 1 annual report 2 daily newspaper 3 company newsletter 4 software manual 5 trade journal 6 travel guide

Ex 4 1-D 2-B 3-A 4-C

Ex 5 1-C 2-A 3-E 4-D 5-F 6B

Ex 6 rose climbed changing accelerating developed move grow

Ex 7 1-C 2-D 3-F 4-A 5-B 6-E

Ex 8 1-E (leaving University. She joined......) 2-F (second half of the year. However, sales fell......) 3-A (of the fare. Short trips.....) 4-C (in technology. Of course, this is.......) 5-D (page number. Even to.....) 6-B (in the economy. Property shares...)

Ex 9 Steve - "Eastern Europe, a Business Guide" Gina - "Fight to Win" Lisa - "When the Chips are Down"

Ex 10 1 the stock market crash 2 a top clothing retailer 3 a business guide 4 in charge of a retail group

5 find your way around   6 a leading company   7 a must for everyone   8 set up a business   9 a share portfolio
10 competitive business climate

UNIT 44

Ex 1 1-B   2-D   3-A   4-C   5-F   6-E
Ex 3 1-T   2-F   3-F   4-T   5-F   6-F   7-T   8-F
Ex 4 position......complaining......boss......negative......easily.. ....watch......excuse....traffic
Ex 5 1 Mr Rumour 2 Ms Indecisive 3 Mr Late   4 Ms Complainer 5 Mr Right 6 Mr Angry
Ex 6 1 by   2 on   3 at   4 for   5 in   6 on   7 in   8 behind

UNIT 45

Ex 2 Time-management should be taken more seriously as a more effective use of time will make employees
more efficient and will lead to less time being wasted.
Ex 3 final week......reviewing......useful advice.......working day.........most efficient......on the
phone........Spend........once or twice
Ex 4 1 decided-concluded   2 out of date-obsolete   3 machinery-equipment 4 aim-purpose
5 workforce-staff   6 unimportant-trivial
Ex 5 1 senior managers   2 the three-day seminar 3 office staff   4 improve productivity   5 the business press
6 working day   7 Prague-based   8 effective time management   9 the first stage of the plan   10 deal with
problems
Ex 6 1 invest your money   2 saves me a lot of time   3 waste a lot of time   4 have the time   5 spend less money
6 make as much money

UNIT 46

Ex 1 1-A/C 2-B 3-B/C 4-A 5-B
Ex 2 1 enough time   2 monitor the progress of   3 proper facilities   4 language teachers 5 language course
6 more money
Ex 3 1 deal in English   2 land a contract   3 pick up some French   4 rely on managers' efforts   5 take the case
of   6 grow frustrated   7 deal with correspondence   8 assess language needs
Ex 4 No. 4 is the most acccurate summary.

UNIT 47

Ex 1 1-C   2-A   3-D   4-B
Ex 2 The original headline is "TRAVEL POLICY CUTS COSTS".
Ex 3 1-F 2-T 3-F 4-T 5-F 6-F 7-T 8-F
Ex 4 1 travel and entertainment budget   2 multi-national   3 major clients   4 regular trips   5 feasible option
6 major clients   7 a feasible option   8 multi-nationals   9 regular trips abroad   10 travel and entertainment
budget

UNIT 48

Ex 2 A-7   B-6   C-1   D-5   E-2   F-8   G-9   H-3   I-4
Ex 4 1 They now allow employees to wear more informal clothes.   2 The change was introduced gradually.
3 Dirty or untidy clothes are not allowed. Some employees still have to dress more formally.   4 Mr Rodriguez
found that most American companies allowed some degree of informal dress. 5 No, they don't. 6 He arrived at
work to find some shirts on his desk.